MW00629119

Journey to a Joyful Life

An ALS-Inspired Treasury of Life Lessons

By Craig Dierksheide

ISBN 978-0-578-34549-9

Grand Strand
Press

Dedication

I would like to dedicate this book to those who are battling ALS, with the hope that a cure can be found in the near future.

Table of Contents

Preface

Chapter 1 – Git 'Er Done!   1

Chapter 2 – You're Nothing Without a Goal   11

Chapter 3 – Track Your Progress!   29

Chapter 4 – What They Don't Teach You in School   41

Chapter 5 – Failure Is the ONLY Option!   57

Chapter 6 – Balance Is the Key to a Happy Life   73

Chapter 7 – Where's Your Bucket List?   83

Chapter 8 – Choose Your Friends Wisely   89

Chapter 9 – The Secret of Living Is Giving   99

Chapter 10 – Look at How Lucky You Are   107

Chapter 11 – Get Your Life Right with God...or Else!   115

Acknowledgements

I would first like to thank my beautiful wife Katie for putting up with me and all my crazy ideas over the past thirty four years of marriage, and especially for being my caregiver for the past three years. It hasn't been easy for her, but she's always been there for me through all the good times and the challenging times.

To my four children, Jake, Anna, Matt, and Paul. My greatest accomplishments. No success or achievement I have accomplished in my life compares to how proud I am of my kids.

A special thanks to my daughter Anna who helped me edit this book from start to finish. I never could have done it without her. I would also like to thank my son Paul for his hard work on designing the cover of the book.

To my long-lost cousin Beth, "Elizabeth," "Liz," Hazel for her publishing skills in getting me over the finish line to format and publish this book and expose it to the world.

I would like to acknowledge Dr. Richard Bedlack and his assistant Stacey Asnani at the Duke University Department of Neurology. They were very helpful in guiding me through the various stages of this disease in monthly visits and telehealth calls since the start of COVID.

I would also like to thank Brett Vowles and Jody Crawford from the South Carolina ALS Association for organizing webinars, fundraising, and monthly Zoom calls with other people fighting ALS in South Carolina. Their knowledge and work ethic have helped tremendously in battling this disease.

I hope my life lessons will make someone's "Journey to a Joyful Life" a little smoother.

Preface

In November of 2019, I was given six months to live. Here I am today in 2022, alive and still cheating death.

I recall the day when I was diagnosed with ALS, I was in total disbelief. Before I tell you about how I felt about being diagnosed with a rare disease called ALS, I think I should give you a little introduction of myself and this damned disease. I sometimes think I should not be too harsh with ALS, though. This disease has lived with me for a while now and has let me live, at least until now.

ALS or Amyotrophic Lateral Sclerosis is a disease of the nervous system that silently affects nerve cells in the brain and spinal cord, causing loss of muscle control.

When I was diagnosed with ALS in 2018, I was told that the average lifespan for a person with ALS is two to five years, but some people live for decades. ALS affects everybody differently. I am not letting this horrible disease take me until I'm ready!

I am grateful that I have achieved a lot in life. I have a beautiful family, and I was living the life many people dream of. There is a lot I want to give back to the world, including my secrets to a happy and successful life. I never thought I would ever write a book, or perhaps it was somewhere in the back of my mind, but after I found out about my illness, I knew I had to do it now.

With my condition, there are many challenges, but the one thing I could do was still type on my phone. So, as difficult and challenging as it was going to be, I thought why not put a document together that perhaps might help someone or, if not, will give a few a little hope and a will to fight if they are facing their own challenges in life. I am sitting here in my wheelchair, typing this on my cell phone, using the side of my thumb to write this book, letter by letter, word by word, paragraph by paragraph, chapter by chapter on my Samsung S8+, using Samsung Notes!

I am on a ventilator 24/7, I can't do things without my wheelchair, and I sometimes sound like I am holding my nose while I speak (I still sound sexy, though). Jokes aside, I would like to kick start this book by giving out my gratitude. First of all, I am thankful to this sickness, for it has caused me to laser focus on countless things that I previously overlooked or didn't have time for.

I am grateful that I was born in a great country like America and was raised by two great parents. I was lucky enough that I was able to find mentors and partners who helped me build an incredible life for myself and my family; I can't thank them enough. I am grateful for the hundreds of people — family, extended family, and friends — who made themselves available for porch visits, sent cards and texts, brought meals, and all the other things that have helped me get through the past three years. You can't convince me that people are bad. They have been incredible. I am beyond thankful for my supportive and amazing wife and unbelievably awesome kids who spent months at a time helping take care of me while working remotely.

I am also grateful for the time I was given on this Earth, although I may miss out on the fourth quarter. I look forward to the next stop in eternity.

I can go on and on about how grateful I am. Also, know that I am grateful to each one of my readers and wish you all the best of everything.

Chapter 1: Git 'Er Done!

"Life is a story. It's full of chapters. And the beauty of life is that not only do you get to choose how you interpret each chapter, but your interpretation writes the next chapter. It determines whether it's comedy or tragedy, fairy tale or horror story, rags-to-riches, or riches-to-rags. You can't control the events that happen to you, but you can control your interpretation of them. So why not choose the story that serves your life the best?"

— Kevin Hart, I Can't Make This Up: Life Lessons

For the past few months, a lot of people have told me that I should write a book. It made me wonder why they even suggested writing a book in the first place. Then a thought occurred to me that perhaps they do not want me to feel useless or incapable of doing things while I am in a wheelchair. I also thought these people knew I was always on the go, and a person like me can't just sit around and do nothing because they have developed some disease. I thought about what they said and considered many things like: What do I even know about writing a book? Is my life really that exciting to have the story preserved in a book? Numerous excuses entered my mind that made me question whether I had the ability to write a book.

Things like:
- I have ALS!
- I'm dying!
- I'm on a ventilator!
- I can't eat anymore!
- I'm in a wheelchair!
- My fingers don't work!
- My legs don't work!
- I don't have the energy!
- I'm too old!

Then suddenly, one day I said to myself, "STOP MAKING EXCUSES!!!" It was true; they were all excuses, which I realized right after I began writing this book. It took some effort; to be honest, it is difficult to type while you are in a wheelchair. I sometimes needed help, but none of the reasons were big enough for me to entirely drop the idea of writing this book. The first step towards failure is the CAN'T DO attitude. If you put forth your efforts and lose, you are still a winner for trying. I have learned the hard way; you've got to take a step forward, even if you're afraid to fail, because action overcomes fear.

My name is Craig Dierksheide, and I turned sixty-three years old on March 19th, 2021. I couldn't believe it at first. Where has life gone? I look back and see it all flashing in front of my eyes. One of my favorite pastimes these days is re-living the best moments of my life, taking a walk down memory lane, and reminiscing over the good times. I recall my journey to the top, the day I met my wife, Katie, and then the day I married her, and when I became a father. Now I have time to appreciate how beautiful those moments were.

I was diagnosed with ALS on September 11th, no not THAT September 11th, but September 11th, 2018. The average life expectancy of the disease is two to five years from diagnosis. A year and a couple of months into the disease, I was told by my doctor at the ALS Clinic at Duke on November 5th, 2019 that based on my diagnosis and the deterioration of my breathing I probably had six months to live! Say WHAAAAT!? That put my demise in May 2020! By now, my life should have been over, finished, done as per the doctor's diagnosis.

That was what made my nights restless and sleepless after the initial days of diagnosis. I had gotten an estimated time of death, and it was dangling over my head, coming sooner rather than later. How could I sleep knowing that? That's the strangest thing about death, you always think you are ready, but you are never ready. Who would want to leave their loved ones behind? Who would want to know that this is probably the last time they're seeing the faces of their loved ones? No amount of good-byes would ever be enough. Anyway, I decided to make the most of every day with the ones I had left. The doctor predicted I would live until May 2020... It's May 2021...and guess what, I'm still here! It makes me wonder if there is a reason why?

On a lighter note, that same doctor told me a couple of months later that I must have been in great shape before ALS as my progress was moving along well. I said to myself, "Well, how much faith can I put in this guy? He's 0 for 2!"

How would your life change if you were told YOU had six months to live? How much would you try to cram into those six months? What would you do? What would you experience? Who would you make peace with? Where would you go?

How do you know how much time you have left? We all think we are invincible and will live to a ripe old age, enjoy the golden years that we deserve after a lifetime of hard work, but some-times we don't even have six months! None of us know, so...GIT 'ER DONE! If someone had asked me before ALS, I wouldn't even have thought about how much time I had left. I had a wonderful life, not that I don't have it now, but you know what I mean. I am progressing well; I am trying to be as strong as I can, but I know that with what I am experiencing right now, no-body can be sure of anything. Life is unpredictable and nobody knows for certain what tomorrow will bring. We lay out a five-year-plan for ourselves, but then life happens, and all of our plans fall flat.

The truth is: none of us know, but one thing for sure is that we all have the same exit strategy, although it doesn't come with a timeline. If only we all had an end date for our demise, life would be so much simpler! So, it's important to make every day on this Earth count. My motto is to make others feel good, help others, and be kind. That is the only thing that matters to me, apart from leaving a legacy for my children. I am pretty sure that they have learned quite a few things from their father, but the most important thing I want them to learn from me is that life is short, live it to its fullest, and don't sweat the small stuff. Ask yourself, will it really matter in five minutes, five hours, five days or five years from now? If it won't, then forget about it and move on.

It's true that as you get older, time seems to go faster and faster. I can remember my grandmother sitting in her rocking chair when I was a small boy expounding on how fast the years were going by when we visited her every summer. "Another year in the books" she'd say, or "you're back so soon?" It was as if it had only been a week since I had seen her previously.

One of my favorite sayings on how fast time flies is by Rudyard Kipling.

If you can fill the unforgiving minute
With sixty seconds' worth of distance run,
Yours is the Earth and everything that's in it,
And – which is more – you'll be a Man, my son!

from the poem "If" by Rudyard Kipling

Since I was diagnosed two and a half years ago it seems like the weeks are going by so quickly, it's Monday then Friday, Monday then Friday. I text my seventy-three year old mentor every Thursday as a running joke with a message like "Holy sh#&, do you know what day tomorrow is? It's FRIDAY...again!!!" I can't even imagine how fast time must be going for him at his age! (I just had to put that in there in case he ever reads this book.)

I have my own theory on why life seems to go fast as you get older. Think about it! When you are two years old, one year is half your life! But when you're eighty-seven years old, one year is only 1/87th of your life. Time is almost irrelevant. Another Monday is just like the previous 4,524 Mondays you've experienced in your life! I don't know if that's the case or not, but something is making my life go by like a rocket. Anyway, that's my story and I'm sticking to it.

I don't know if this book will mean anything to anyone or be a bestseller, but I truly believe I'm still here for a reason, and as you will see throughout this book, there are a lot of "things" that have happened in the last two and a half years and I think those "things" have happened for a reason. I will explain more of why I feel this way throughout this book.

The key take-away from this book will be different for every reader, depending on their age and status in life. Still, overall, the purpose of this book is to inspire you, to motivate you, to make you rich, to make you laugh, cry, and maybe even give you some life perspective from someone who has seen a few things, done a few things, lived a full life, and whose sands of time are quickly slipping through the hourglass of life!

Buckle up, buttercup...here we go!

Stop Making Excuses
Let's talk some business now. I really admire you for picking up this book written by someone who has had a lot of life experiences. If you knew how much just one or two of these ideas could change your life, I think you will find this book very educational. What is a story without a lesson, after all? I am a firm believer that wisdom is acquired by overcoming challenges or difficult situations. Learning from the experiences of others is less painful than learning those lessons by trial and error.

The first thing I want you all to learn is that making excuses will never get you anywhere. If you make excuses only to avoid doing something, then you don't really want it bad enough in the first place. Your dream life is never going to manifest itself if you keep thinking about what may go wrong.

Sometimes we are hesitant to reach out and ask others for help for various reasons. I would never be who I am today if I weren't willing to ask for help or if my mentors weren't willing to share their wisdom with me. There is no shame in asking questions if you don't know the answer. Educating yourself is the key to success. Embrace the advice that others pass on to you. You never know what might help you when you need it. We make excuses for ourselves when other people succeed and we don't. We blame failure on other individuals, occasions, and conditions. Excuses are reasons we make up to guard our conduct, to defer making a move, or basically as a method for ignoring responsibility.

It doesn't matter how old you are. Going after what you want and being successful can happen at any age. Mozart started composing at age five, while the sculptor Michelangelo completed St. Peter's Basilica in his late seventies.

Ponder over the people whose achievements you respect and how old they were when they accomplished it. You can do almost anything regardless of your age. If you have a passion and a will to do something, and if you have done everything within your capacity to make it happen, chances are that you will achieve it. The harder you work the luckier you get. We all have our reasons to come up with excuses. Some are afraid of failures; others are way too absorbed with worrying about "what ifs." We need to understand that our comfort zone should not become our prison or a hurdle in our success.

I am 63, and I have seen enough of the world to know that any one of you can make it big. I have seen people succeed when no one thought that they could. Trust me, I only preach what I have practiced myself.

The first thing I want you to learn on your road to success is to stop making these useless excuses and go get what you want because you can, and you will!

Chapter 2: You're Nothing Without a Goal

Having reached the golden years of my life, I have arrived at the conclusion that nothing in life comes easy. To achieve what your heart desires, you have to work hard. Really hard. Everyone wants to reach the heights of success, everyone wishes to drive a Mercedes, or wear a $2,000 Armani suit. However, to have all these things and more, all the luxuries of life that you desire, you must come up with a plan and you must work hard towards that plan. If you wish to succeed and reach a commendable position in life, you need to set goals for yourself. You need to define where you want to be in the next three or five years. Without goals you lack direction and focus. Setting goals not only enables you to take charge of your life's direction, but it also provides you with a benchmark for determining if you are on the correct path towards success.

No one should underestimate why setting goals is important and doing periodic reassessments is even more important. Your future, the way your life will become, depends solely on you and the actions you will take in your life. You and you alone are responsible for shaping your life into what you want it to become. No one and nothing else will be responsible for your life. When you were a student in school your teacher told you each day what to do to get good results and later contribute to society in a positive way. At your job, your boss tells you each day what to do, and then expects good results to enrich the company's profits. However, when it comes to your own life it is up to you to give yourself a set of expectations to improve your own life, as well as the lives of those around you, and continually grow in all aspects of your life.

Do you know in this very moment what exactly you want to achieve in your life? If you don't, how will you know if and when you achieved it? The difference between dreams and goals is that dreams are only thoughts, while goals are step-by-step plans on how to achieve the end result. Everything that came into existence started as a simple thought in someone's mind. In your mind today are all the plans, dreams, and ideas for your future: who you want to become, where you want to be, what you will achieve, how you will enrich your own life and the lives of those around you.

To achieve goals you must know what it is you want to do with your life. Do not allow your goals to remain solely in your thoughts, but rather write them down, for anything that is written down, and in front of you on a daily basis will have a better chance of being accomplished. Reading and re-reading your goals will allow you to pursue and intensively realize them, and also will create an external feeling of urgency: those two traits will not be valid if your goals remain only in your thoughts.

Get a pen and a piece of paper and write down one hundred goals you want to achieve in your life. Thinking of one hundred life goals may seem like a lot, but there's a reason for this, as you'll discover below. Your goals should be in various domains of life: personal, professional, educational, spiritual, financial, contributions to society through your God-given talents, places you want to visit, people you want to meet, and so on. While writing your goals, make sure that they only pertain to you and you alone. For instance, "My friend will change and become the person I want her to be," isn't a valid goal since you have no control over others, but only over yourself and your own actions, and so the above is only a wish. On the contrary, "I will accept my friend just the way she is, and will stop judging her," is a valid goal, since it describes something, you can do - start accepting and cease being judgmental. This kind of goal will ensure your growth.

Be SMART

A useful way to evaluate your goals is by using the SMART concept. The first-known use of this acronym appeared in the November 1981 issue of *Management Review* by George T. Doran*, and it's associated with Peter Drucker's "management by objectives concept." Make sure all of your goals are SMART:

S = Specific

M = Measurable

A = Attainable

R = Realistic

T = Timely

Be specific.

Instead of "Someday I will go back to school," write "I will enroll in college for the fall semester and will take the following classes... "

Measurable.

Instead of "I will study some Portuguese," write "I will learn Portuguese until I'll be able to easily carry on a conversation three months from now."

Attainable.

Instead of "I'll fly to the moon for my next vacation," write "I'll visit Australia two years from today's date."

* George T. Doran in *Management Review*, 70 (11): pp 35–36

Realistic.

Instead of "I'll win the lottery and buy that new car I've always wanted," write "I'll save up (specific amount) towards a down payment for my dream car."

Timely.

Instead of "I'll work out at the gym eight hours every day to lower my blood pressure by the end of this week," write "I'll go to the gym three times a week and lower my blood pressure by the end of next month."

Make sure that your goals can be reached within different time frames: two months, six months, one year, five, or ten years. If all your goals can be accomplished within the next three months it indicates that you aren't challenging yourself enough, and would rather play it safe and avoid stepping outside of your comfort zone. Dream big and set goals for yourself that will require lots of work, time, perseverance, determination, and diligence. The journey will not be easy, but I can assure you that it will make your life one that is interesting, happy, and worth living.

Carry your list with you, read it often, and upon accomplishing a goal do not just cross it out (it is not a shopping list, or a daily to-do list), but with a red marker write "Victory" over it. With time you'll be able to see all the things you've achieved in your life up to that point. Seeing all of those Victory notes will inspire you, make you realize your own value, and it will help you believe in yourself to continue striving for future endeavors. As soon as you accomplish one goal, immediately write another one at the end of your list, so you will always have a list of one hundred goals.

Most people go through their days working at the same job and doing the same mundane tasks to get a paycheck at the end of the week. They go home on Friday and get up and repeat the same pattern again on Monday. C'mon man, you live in the greatest country in the world. Opportunities are endless. Don't waste your life making someone else rich, do it for yourself! I'll let you in on a little secret: *it doesn't take age to retire, it takes money!*

You can take an early retirement at the age of thirty if you have a few million dollars, or you can keep working until your bones creak as you move! It's your choice.

Setting and reaching goals in your life is not an easy process. It's so much easier to live the same mundane life day in and day out. Nothing is risked, but also nothing is gained. However, I can assure you that in the very moment when you decide to take the first step and reach for a goal, your life will never be the same, and each day will be filled with excitement, joy and happiness. The rewards will be much greater than the sacrifice, and your life will be forever transformed. Remember that a mind once stretched never returns to its original dimensions.

Setting Goals in Different Areas

Most people have no idea where they're heading, so they aren't aware of where they'll end up. Are you one of them? The good news is, you can fix this right now. Only 3% of people have written goals and only 20% have any goals at all. Less than 1% of the population have goals written down and look at them on a daily basis. So, do you want to be ahead of 80% of people? Here are some examples of different types of goals:

- Spiritual Goals
- Financial & Material Goals
- Business & Career Goals
- Personal Relationship & Social Goals
- Health & Recreational Goals
- Personal Development & Growth Goals

You may also have your own goals you're already working on, but if you don't, then this is a great place to start! You can apply these principles to any of the goal categories shared previously, or anything else you're working on, whether it is running a marathon, learning something new, or even writing a book.

Flying Lessons

Let me tell you a personal story about what happens when you have a goal. I always wanted to learn to fly an airplane. When I was twenty-nine years old, I secretly snuck around and got my pilot's license without telling my wife. Her nephew's high school graduation was coming up that spring, and I wanted to surprise her and fly her to her nephew's graduation. After several months of ground school, weekly flying lessons, and a written exam, I was able to obtain a license so I could fly. The same day I got my pilot's license, I rented an airplane for the weekend from the local flying school, and the next day my wife and I flew from Myrtle Beach to Tallahassee for her nephew's graduation.

GOALS! Something you want, a defined time frame, and a plan of action. Can you imagine the excitement, fear, and exhilaration in setting that one goal to take my wife to see her nephew's graduation come true? Yes, we made it to Tallahassee on time for the graduation and yes, in case you're wondering, my wife does love me and has for the past thirty-four years! The joyous expression on my wife's face is still lovingly preserved in my memory. My goal served two purposes - it enriched me with a feeling of accomplishment, and it made my wife ecstatic.

Remember, however, that since we are all connected, each decision you make, each plan you decide to pursue (or even more importantly not pursue), will have a positive or negative impact on the people around you. Just think for a moment: you are here today reading these words, because you had a thought of enriching your life and the lives of others and as that thought became reality, now, at this very moment your own life will be impacted because of that one decision. Therefore let your plans be wise, serving the good of humanity, and making a positive difference in your own and in others' lives. Talk about faith! Getting into an airplane with somebody who just got their pilot's license the same day, and flying from Myrtle Beach to Tallahassee takes an awful lot of faith. We'll talk more about that in another chapter.

Here is an example of what happens when you don't have a goal, plan, or a time-frame! A couple years after I took flying lessons, I bought a Cessna 172 airplane. Once again, I forgot to tell my wife that I was purchasing the airplane. (She loves surprises, what can I say?) My business partner, Hampton, used to live in Columbia, South Carolina. One day I flew over to pick him up and bring him back to Myrtle Beach. I thought I would just wing it (no pun intended!) and fly without a timeframe or a flight plan. I had driven back-and-forth many times on the highway between Myrtle Beach and Columbia, South Carolina.

Shortly after we took off from Columbia and started to gain altitude, Hampton looked over at me and said, "Craig, you're flying right over the top of Fort Jackson!"

I replied, "We can't be, it's a restricted area. Look, right below us is Highway 378 and we're heading east, so I have to be going towards Myrtle Beach."

He looked at me with a puzzled look in his eyes and said, "Craig, first of all, that's not 378. I spent over a year of my life at Fort Jackson for boot camp. I think I know what it looks like."

Lo and behold, I was way off target and right over Fort Jackson, South Carolina in restricted air space. For the record, the mistake was not life threatening, but I did have visions of two F-15s flying up on either side of me and escorting me out of the area. That's what happens when you don't have a goal, and when you don't know where you're going or when you're going to get there.

Moving to Another State

Here's another example of a good goal. I was living in Tallahassee after graduating from Florida State University back in 1979. I absolutely loved my college years at Florida State. It just so happened that I arrived at FSU in the fall of 1976, the same semester as Bobby Bowden, the great football coach. After living in Tallahassee for several years after graduating college, I decided it was time to move on. When I was growing up my family lived in Ohio, Illinois, Michigan, Connecticut and even Valencia, Venezuela in South America. I decided to go to college in the South because I hadn't experienced the South by that point in my life. Makes sense, right? After graduating from college and working in Tallahassee for a few years, things weren't working out so well for me career-wise. Tallahassee is a government town and I was looking for something in business. I decided to leave.

I spoke with my parents and told them that I wanted to move to the Carolinas, either North or South. I wanted to have a little change of seasons and I loved that southern accent. I dated a couple of North Carolina girls in college and during my single days in Myrtle Beach and that accent melted my heart like an ice cube in a glass of sweet tea on an August afternoon.

Coincidentally, my father had attended an Advanced Management Program at Harvard with Mary Jolley, a lady from Charleston who was the head of Human Resources at Trident Technical College. I was a member of the Pi Kappa Phi fraternity and figured I could do a job hunt for a week in Charleston while staying with my Dad's friends, and a week in Raleigh at North Carolina State University at the Pi Kappa Phi fraternity house on campus. I had two weeks of vacation coming up and I had ample time on my hands. I wouldn't have to take any time off. I have a goal, I have a destination, and I have a time frame!

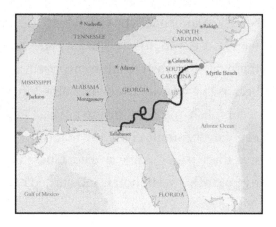

I'll never forget the scene, driving over the bridge going to Charleston, and looking out over the marina. It was quite different from Tallahassee, and I thought it would be a fun place to live. I arrived at my father's friend's home, rang the doorbell, and this beautiful southern woman came to the door. She said, "You must be Dale's boy! From now on, my house is your house too." She cooked me a hearty meal. After a delicious homemade southern dinner of chicken bog, butter beans, cornbread, and peach cobbler for dessert, I started looking through the "Help Wanted" section of the paper, planning my attack, working towards my goal of finding a new career. But it wasn't only about a career: I wanted to find a new direction in life.

The next morning I was ready to go. I was up and out the door by 7:00 a.m. I was on a mission and I had a timeline! I started in the phonebook and reached out to every temporary employment agency in town. Then I started calling the phone numbers given in the Help Wanted ads in the paper to see if anybody was looking to hire. Once I was done with that, I had a little free time on my hands so I went to the main Piggly Wiggly warehouse located in Charleston and hopped up on the loading dock outside in search of someone who could help me. I met the manager of the warehouse, and needless to say, he was a little surprised to see me there. No, he wasn't a little surprised. That is an understatement because he was amazed. I explained to him what I was trying to accomplish and what my goal was. I talked him into giving me a list of every single company that calls on him at that warehouse. It was three pages single spaced. Guess what I did? I didn't quit at five o'clock, I went home and started calling that list. On that list were vendors like Quaker Oats, Procter & Gamble, Nestlé, and more. Literally every single company that you find in a supermarket. When I got a hold of somebody on the telephone, I politely explained to them what my goals were, what I was trying to accomplish, and my time frame. I just kept going one by one down the list. I didn't quit, I didn't give up. When I was told they didn't have anything available at that time, I just kept going. My goal

was not only to have one job lined up by the end of those two weeks, but to have many jobs lined up by the end of the week!

The next day I was up and out again by 7:00 a.m. After making calls all throughout the day, that afternoon I decided I would walk around the campus of the College of Charleston, which is where my college fraternity Pi Kappa Phi was founded. I decided to walk around the campus while all the other businesses were closed to see if I could find somebody at the fraternity house or with a Pi Kappa Phi jersey. Another reason for walking around the campus was that I might run into someone from Pi Kappa Phi who lived around the area, and whose parents perhaps owned a local business and were looking to hire. I would take a shot at it. As I was walking through campus I noticed a building that said "Career Center" and I decided see if they had any jobs in there that would interest me. I went inside and walked up to the counter, asked the clerk if I could interview for the jobs that were posted on 3x5 index cards and thumb-tacked to the bulletin board. She looked at me with some confusion, and asked me if I went to the College of Charleston since the colors on my fraternity jersey did not match their school colors. I explained that I was from Tallahassee looking to move to Charleston or Raleigh and was in need of a job. She got a smile on her face and said in a very polite way, "We usually reserve those jobs for the students who graduate from College of Charleston!" But she looked at me with her big brown eyes and asked the question that changed the course of my life, "Do you know anything about video games?"

As a matter of fact, I did know a few things about video games! My college roommate had opened an arcade back in the early days of Ms. Pacman. We went every night after class and played games, unjammed the quarters, and fixed the monitors. I explained this to the lady and she said, "That's funny because I just received a call from a gentleman who has sixteen arcades in the Charleston area and he's looking for some help." I asked her if she would share his phone number with me and I set up an interview for the next day. Little did I know that phone call was going to be a life-changer.

At the interview, the gentleman offered me a job on the spot. I did not accept his offer immediately as I still wanted to look at my options and go to Raleigh to see what it had to offer. Had I not gone to the College of Charleston, walked around the campus, stumbled upon the Career Center, asked that lady if I could interview for a job, and asked for the phone number, the whole course of my life and career would have taken a totally different direction. In life, there is no such thing as chance, only causation. Things don't happen because you got lucky. Sure, luck does play a role, but your actions have a massive influence on the way things turn out for you.

Creating Your Own Chances

You can do the same thing in your life with whatever goal you desire. If you want to run a marathon and you're out of shape, you might have to give yourself a little more time. You could start by running a half marathon. It would probably not be wise to go out and run a full race next weekend if you're out of shape and have never run one in your life. Start by looking at the internet for upcoming marathons in your area and pick a date that seems reasonable for the amount of time you have to prepare. Break the goal down by the number of weeks before the marathon. Now that you know the number of weeks you have, break down each individual week and what you want to accomplish during that week. The beauty of this is you really don't have to specify the details, but you must know where to start. If the half-marathon is 13.1 miles and there's a race twenty weeks from now, you better be able to run 6.5 miles in ten weeks. Break down what you need to accomplish each week based on your goals, and then look at your achievements and see if you did what you needed to do. But you better start today.

Once you've written a list of goals, you must check your progress every day! Do you have a goal, a time frame, and what you need to do to accomplish that goal on a daily basis? If you get three weeks into the process and find out you're only able to run a mile, then you need to readjust your goals for a marathon and choose a more achievable date. The satisfaction you receive from accomplishing this task will be something you remember the rest of your life.

One more quick personal example. Everybody wants to lose weight, but nobody ever does. Why is that? What are the reasons? I believe the reasons are that people don't choose a target weight, set a date for when they want to achieve the weight, and they don't write down their progress as they go along. I lost 50 pounds in five months. I set a goal to go from 300 to 250 pounds in twenty weeks. I knew I had to lose at least 2.5 pounds a week. Do you

know how I did it without even struggling? I took a piece of graph paper, and wrote down what my weight should be at the end of each week. Then I broke each week down into two parts figuring I needed to lose 1.25 pounds every three or four days. I tracked my progress on a daily basis. I recorded my weight twice a week on that spreadsheet and followed my progress. It was very motivating when I was ahead of schedule by a pound or two, and I knew I had to work a little harder if I was behind a pound or two. As I watched the pounds fall off on a daily basis it became very exciting and I was inspired to keep going. Five months later, I weighed 245 pounds and could easily have gotten to 200 pounds had the doctor not diagnosed my ALS and prohibited me from losing weight. My goals followed the SMART model for achievement.

I wish you those feelings of satisfaction on your way to accomplishing your goals. I hope you will become a light in your world, a light that will shine brightly on your family, church, city, and even world community, that you become a positive force of change in the world, the kind of change that will improve the lives of many people in your immediate surroundings and across the globe. It is already within your power, but only you can make the decision to use it. I hope your decision will be "yes!"

Do not give up if something is difficult, or does not go your way, because your character is not shaped in times when everything goes as planned, but rather in times of adversity, when nothing goes as you want it. If you have to find alternative ways of achieving your goals, that's when perseverance, diligence, and determination will play the biggest role. Use those moments to shape your character and to go on despite difficulties. Don't allow anyone to tell you, "This can't be done," but instead find a way to achieve your goal. Go over, go under, go around, or go through, but never give up.

Chapter 3: Track Your Progress!

"Every day you spend drifting away from your goals is a waste not only of that day, but also of the additional day it takes to regain lost ground."   - Ralph Marston

This is where things get really exciting! You're on the road to somewhere and your destination is calling you. You have goals, time frames, and a map written down guiding you in the right direction, which should be very powerful in itself.

"A journey of a thousand miles begins with a single step."
A Chinese proverb

Many people may call this 'just a quote' and ignore it, or would not care to ponder over it. But if you think about the saying, you will learn how true it is. I find that the biggest problem with most people is they want to accomplish something like losing weight or getting rich, but it is a distant thought for them. They want to do it, but they don't have a starting or ending point, nor do they have a solid plan in hand. I've heard many people say, "I want to lose twenty pounds, and I'll start right after the holidays." The holidays come and go, and nothing happens except that they indulge themselves a little more during the holiday season because they were thinking about the diet they had planned to start after the holidays. The twenty pounds are still there, but they blame it on the delicious turkey and pumpkin pie, of course.

The key is to set meaningful goals for yourself, the ones you actually want to accomplish from the bottom of your heart. If and when you want something badly enough, you're sufficiently motivated to pick yourself up and work towards its fulfillment.

Accountability

Work on your goal with another person. This is called *accountability* and it's an extremely powerful method to ensure you accomplish your goals. It's used by life coaches and in mastermind groups. If you can find someone who has goals similar to yours, it's a great idea to have an accountability partner. They don't need to be doing exactly what you're doing but it is a good idea to have a similar time frame so one of you doesn't get the short end of the stick and end up being the accountability partner long after the other person has finished their task! You can keep each other accountable with a simple phone call, text, in person or however you think is best. Having an accountability partner will go a long way towards helping you stay on track to achieve your goals.

Any person, young or old, must have a definitive start date and end date by which they wish to achieve their target. Once you have a timeframe, the real key here is to break the goal down into bite size, achievable pieces. The smaller the bites, the better and easier it is to achieve your goal. Just like my weight loss example! Here's another scenario: let's say you're 25-years old, and you want to be a millionaire by the age of 65. A twenty-five year old would need to save approximately $400 a month to achieve a $1 million balance by age sixty-five, assuming a 7% annualized return on the investment. While that may seem like a lot, workers with a 401(k) may receive automatic contributions to their retirement plan from their employer. When you break your goal down on a monthly basis, it becomes more realistic and achievable.

There are all kinds of calculators on the internet that can help you set monthly financial goals. Just think how exciting it would be when you're forty years old and you look back to that very first $400 you invested. Look at the chart of where you stand at present, compare it with where you should be, and figure out if you need to add a little more money each month or if you're ahead of the game. Either way, you'll know exactly where you are, and you will be a millionaire in the golden years of your life, enjoying a martini or two in Barbados. By the way, here's how an average American is doing when it comes to saving for retirement by age groups.

Americans in their 20s: $16,000
Americans in their 30s: $45,000
Americans in their 40s: $63,000
Americans in their 50s: $117,000
Americans in their 60s: $172,000 *

Pretty scary, huh?

* Survey by the Transamerica Center for Retirement Studies,
https://www.synchronybank.com

A good friend of mine started tracking his net worth quarterly since right after he graduated college. He is very conservative in his investing and has a net worth of over $10 million. Now that's absolutely impressive. He had a small landscaping business that he owned but along the way he invested in real estate. He ran his business, worked on delinquent tax sales, traded stocks, and work with a variety of real estate investments. He sold his business and retired in his forties, but continued to create income through his investments. As far as having a job or going to a job is concerned, he'll never do anything he doesn't want to do again. He won't have to be bossed around, because he chose the smart path and became his own boss and gained financial independence.

I don't exactly know how the subconscious mind works, as I am no psychologist, but I can tell you from experience that if you remain focused on a goal and you really aspire to achieve that goal in life, the whole Universe conspires to give it to you. Your hard work and efforts are never in vain. When you are true to yourself, and you work towards your goal with the utmost honesty and dedication, you eventually accomplish it. Destiny works in mysterious ways. Whatever is on top of your mind, whatever you're looking for, it actually manifests right in front of you. When opportunities present themselves, you are able to recognize those opportunities. You get what you want, however, it goes without saying that the struggle and the waiting is exhausting.

Have you ever heard "out of sight, out of mind"? That's how it works when you have a goal and write it down. When something is constantly on your mind, your motivation is increased by visualizing mental pictures. It reinforces what you are attempting to do, and suddenly opportunities begin to appear out of nowhere.

Working on Short Term Goals

Suppose you have always wanted to read the Bible but it's very long—and let's face it, it doesn't exactly read like a good romance novel. An average Bible has approximately 1,200 pages. This makes the calculation pretty easy. Let's say that you wish to read it in six months but not on weekends. Each month on average has about 20 weekdays, so each month you would need to read 200 pages. That works out to ten pages a day. Anyone can read ten pages a day. Now chart it, write it down, track it. Did you read your fifty pages this week? Are you ahead or behind? If it's too much, adjust your chart and read five pages a day and finish reading the book in a little over a year.

Another tip to help keep you on track and make following your chart fun is to reward yourself along the way. The harder the task, the bigger the reward. Even if you divide your grand goals into smaller goals, reward yourself on the completion of each one of them. Next time you have something you really want to achieve, use that desire as a motivational tool to practice delayed gratification. If you really want that new dress, tell yourself that after you read those first 100 pages you will buy it and not a page before. This is a great way to keep you motivated and on track, and as a bonus on the side, you will also learn the practice of delayed gratification.

The Seed for My Book

It's been amazing to see how this whole book idea has taken shape. It started with an old friend, Jodie, instant messaging me on Facebook, wondering how I was doing. I didn't even know at that time if she knew about my diagnosis with ALS. She had heard through the grapevine about what was happening to me. After texting back and forth, I told her she should come by for a porch visit. The next day she was standing right in my front door with a smile on her face. We had a nice two-hour visit on the back porch, catching up on kids, life, housing, and more.

This is where things really started to get interesting. I had a funny feeling that night that she returned to my life for a reason, but I had no idea why. The irony of it was that she felt the same thing, that there was a reason that we reconnected via Facebook

The Porch

and followed up with a visit. A couple of days later she called and asked if she could bring a friend by for a porch visit. I told her that she could. The next day she brought Pamela Pyle, a retired doctor-turned-author, who was writing a book titled *A Good Death*. The book was based on her years of experience and knowledge from being a doctor, and inspired by a patient telling her about how she was going to have a "good death."

I had no idea of any of this at the time. We just had a normal porch visit laughing, crying, talking about life, the past, people we knew in common, and about ALS. Just a regular visit with old friends. At the end, I bid them farewell and thought that was the end of it. A pleasant visit that gave me a new friend, for which I will always be grateful.

The Porch

A couple of weeks later, out of the blue, I received an email unexpectedly from Pam with a transcript of her book, *A Good Death*. It was followed up a couple of days later by a fourteen-page story about our porch visit! It was beautifully written, and I was deeply touched. I had no idea I talked that much during our porch visit. Pam mentioned in the email that she wanted to come back for another visit, to which I readily agreed.

During the next visit, Pam and I conversed more deeply on subjects like death, religion, and how my life had changed since my diagnosis. She kept asking me about my legacy! Talk about a deep subject. How would you answer that question? I fumbled around, and I wasn't sure how exactly to respond.

I told her, "I guess my kids are my legacy, or the people I've influenced in life."

Pam kept digging but I never felt like I was giving her what she needed. We did a virtual visit about a week later, with more questions and more vague answers. We hung up, and I still felt the same way that I had felt previously, that I wasn't giving Pam what she was looking for.

A couple of weeks went by, and I had not heard from Pam. I thought that might be the end of our recently built friendship. During those two weeks, my wife organized a surprise birthday party for me. Because of COVID-19, we could not have a traditional birthday party, so instead she decided to host a "drive-by" birthday party. In lieu of gifts we asked people to donate to the South Carolina ALS Association. I planned to match the total contributions collected. It was a very cold day in March, but at least the sun was shining brightly. The party was a huge success! We had around 150 cars come through over a four-hour period. Unbelievable as it may sound, we raised around $3,700 which I matched, and we sent a check to the South Carolina ALS Association for $7,500. The feeling of giving was incredible!

Pam and her husband Scott were invited to the party too, but they had other plans that day and couldn't make it. However, Jodie reached out to Pam to tell her what she missed. That same day I was just about to email Pam and tell her that I was sorry that I had not given her what she was looking for in regards to my legacy, when coincidentally an email from Pam was already in my inbox. The subject of the email read: *So I kept writing and rewriting the ending until your birthday parade made it clear :) Let me know what you think.*

The email read: *I received a text from Jodie. "I visited Craig's birthday parade. His legacy could be seen for miles."*

In my journey of discovering the legacy of others, I am encouraged by the truth that lasting legacy is most often found by the imprint we leave in the lives of others. Mother Theresa so beautifully expressed this principle, "Not all of us can do great things. But we can do small things with great love." You and Katie have built a legacy around this principle and long after we are all gone, that tree will keep blooming!

Attached to the email was the conclusion of the story of my legacy. I sat and read it and cried for minutes like a baby. All of a sudden things became perfectly vivid to me, and I responded to Pam with this text:

Pam, YOU were the reason God put Jodie and I together again! Beautiful job... absolutely BEAUTIFUL!!! You made my meaningless life so much more MEANINGFUL!!! I am somebody! I have done good! I may not have built a hospital in Rwanda like you did, but YOU made me see how I did something to make the World a little bit better place and for that, I am ETERNALLY GRATEFUL!

After reading this short story, I thought it would have so much more meaning if we put pictures with it to make the story come alive. I recruited my daughter, Anna, to do a picture book with photographs of me with my family and friends to illustrate Pam's text. I received the book a couple of weeks later in the mail and it turned out beautifully. It was at that point I had a vision to write this book you are reading now for my legacy to teach people life lessons and raise more money for the South Carolina ALS Association and local charities. How's that for a legacy?

Once I had the vision in mind, I had a goal, the reason I wanted to do it. With a target date of July 4th, 2021. I knew I needed to complete approximately one chapter a week for the next seven weeks. You see how it seems like less of a challenge when you break it down on a weekly basis? You can break it down even further into daily increments and realize you only need to complete about two pages a day. And if I stick to the plan, who knows, on the 4th of July dinner, perhaps I'll be reading my book to my family over the dinner table!

It turns out that writing a book was much more involved than I thought, especially in my condition. Family and friends came to visit, often weeks at a time. Scheduling challenges with getting help in the days I could write, all would make great excuses to not write a book.

However, I didn't give up, I found solutions and revised my timeline. I rehired my administrative assistant Teri, to help me work on the book. The reason I rehired Teri was because as I was leaning forward typing with my thumb on the phone for hours at a time, I realized not only was I getting behind on my goal but I was developing "tech neck" and it was getting harder and harder to hold my head up.

Today is October 4th, 2021 and all chapters are done. Now comes editing, re-writing, and figuring out how to get this book published on Amazon. No excuses, git 'er done.

Do you see what happens when you have a goal and you are willing to do whatever it takes to accomplish that goal? You find creative solutions, and friends come out of nowhere and volunteer to help you accomplish your goal.

◆◆◆◆◆

So there you have it. It was a roundabout way to show you how I arrived at this goal of writing a book, but I wanted to give you an idea of the process that happens and the steps that took place from the initial porch visit right up through today. Tracking your goals is a powerful tool. It is only then we realize that there is always a plan in motion, guiding us to exactly where we are supposed to be, in the exact time frame that has been destined for us.

Chapter 4: What They Don't Teach You in School

I don't think I'm the only one who found those algebra, trigonometry, and calculus classes painstakingly boring. I remember how throughout the class I would wonder about the relevance of the courses and why we needed to study them in the first place. I found them extremely useless, and my opinion still remains the same today. I mean, c'mon, ask yourself, when was the last time you used algebra, trigonometry, or even calculus in life? I don't think anyone ever even touches the course books after graduating from high school.

I know I didn't… so, the question arises, why do school systems spend the time and energy to teach us things that we barely use, that does no good to our lives at all, unless and until we are engineers or astronauts. Why would schools make us learn things that are not going to help us at all with our lives?

Why is it that the most important things that we need to succeed in life aren't taught to us from a tender age? How come our math teacher didn't teach us to balance a checkbook, how to read a stock chart, or how to make an investment in a mutual fund? Did our teachers teach any of us how an annuity works or what a surrender fee is? Nobody ever taught us about saving and investing money in the right places while we were in high school. Imagine all the money we would have saved by now, had we known earlier how to save and invest. Did an instructor ever teach you how to open a brokerage account or set up a 401(k) or a Roth IRA? The most important things needed to live a financially secure life aren't taught to us in school at all. Shouldn't we prioritize teaching the most critical lessons, like how living below your means and investing the difference will take you toward financial independence or early retirement? Why is it that we are not taught to buy real estate and use it to grow our wealth?

We aren't taught to take a break from work, either. We're encouraged to work twenty-four hours a day, seven days a week if we aspire to make a name for ourselves.

It's fascinated me ever since I was a little boy about how rich and famous people became wealthy and how they picked their chosen careers. Look at how many people do what their parents did for a living...they get to do the same job as their father did, or in most cases that is a family business being passed on from one generation to another. But is that what you really want? Everything handed down to you on a silver platter? How would you explore your abilities then? How would you know your limits and what you're capable of? You will never know the things you can do in life until you stretch yourself. You need to step out of your comfort zone and see what's out there. I promise you there is a vast array of opportunities waiting to embrace you with arms wide open. Try out something new, something you've never done before. Learn a new skill, baking, or origami maybe. See how quickly you learn and observe yourself. Does it make you feel creative and happy? If yes, then perhaps you're in the right place. Learn a new language, travel to a land faraway, talk to the locals, and enjoy their cuisines! If you're not inclined to visit a foreign country then explore your own country and see what it has to offer to you. Get enrolled in an internship program. Talk to different people. Learn to respect other people's opinions while respectfully getting yours across. See what floats your boat. My point is that the universe is a gigantic place and there are hundreds of thousands of opportunities for each of us. You just have to look out for them.

It has always amazed me how little time people devote to selecting a career path and seem to give it very little thought. Your career is one of the defining things about you, so it is wise for people to spend more time thinking about it to ensure they make the choice that suits them best. When I lived in South America and we flew home every summer, I would always ask my parents to book me a seat by myself so that I could interview the person sitting next to me. In retrospect, I'm kind of surprised that they allowed me to sit by myself. It was fascinating to ask people what they did for a living and why they did it. It was fun holding a conversation with a complete stranger who did not know me. And I always left the airplane with a new lesson up my sleeve.

On one of the flights, I sat next to a businessman. I asked him where he worked. He said that he worked for the Dana Corporation. I asked him if he knew Carl Hirsch? He looked at me with amazement and said, "Why, yes, he's my boss." I attended a private American school in Venezuela where most of the parents were upwardly mobile middle managers and the Hirsches were good friends of ours. It's a small world. The look on his face was one I will never forget.

The Danger of Debts

Before we talk about investing, let me first give you a warning about credit cards. In this world that we live in, we are bombarded with advertisements talking about how we deserve a new car, to go on a cruise, to wear designer fashions, and the list goes on. A bitter reality of our life is that we are inclined to buy the things we cannot afford to impress the people who don't matter. Let me be very candid with you. You don't deserve anything unless you can afford to pay for it. I am speaking from experience when I tell you this because at one point in my life, I had five credit cards maxed out with thousands of dollars in credit limits. I could not even make the minimum payments and my roommate loaned me three of those credits cards to help me dig my way out of a hole that just kept getting deeper and deeper.

I had to do something completely different so I packed my bags and headed to Charleston to seek new opportunities. I swore the day I left that if there was any way I could get out from underneath the debt and live on less than I was making, I would do everything in my power to make sure I was never in this position again. My debts were having a terrible effect on me because they kept piling up and I had no means to pay them off. As I explained earlier, I thankfully set a new course for my life after moving away from Charleston. One thing led to another, and eventually my financial condition started getting better. I was able to pay off all five credit cards and to this day have never carried a balance since. I have made a cardinal rule about using my credit card: if I can't pay it off at the end of the month, I don't buy it. PERIOD.

Credit card companies can charge up to 23% or more in interest and it doesn't take long to dig a hole you can't get out of. Credit card companies are masters at compound interest and know how to take full advantage of you when you get into financial trouble. Maybe some of you reading this book are in that position right now. If you are, I'll tell you a story that the great Warren Buffett told at the 2020 Berkshire Hathaway annual stockholders meeting.

Warren Buffet shared financial advice with all the attendees, and told us his mantra for personal finances as well. He said, "Avoid using credit cards as a piggy bank." He told a story about an old friend who inherited some money and came to him to ask for his advice on investing. I'm sure she was looking for the next hot stock pick or how she should double her money. "She said I have some money, what should I do with it?" Warren said, "How much do you owe on your credit card?" Buffett recalled, "She said, well I owe X, and I'm paying 18% interest."

"I don't know how to make an 18% return on my money," Buffett added. "If I owed any money at 18%, the first thing I'd do with any money I had, I would pay it off."

"Because paying it off is going to be way better than any investment idea that I've got," he stressed. "And that wasn't what she wanted to hear." Then she asked Warren what her daughter should do with a couple thousand dollars cash and he said, "Have her lend it to you at 18%, if you are willing to pay 18% or whatever it is, I mean she's not going to find a better deal, it doesn't make sense to go through life borrowing money at those rates and be better off. I would suggest to anybody that the first thing they do in life is that they can get something else later on, but don't be paying even 12% to anybody just pay that off. If they disagree with me, come see me and I will be glad to lend them money at that rate." And he chuckled out loud.

Dollar bills are a story of the past now for 60% of Americans, who have now replaced dollar bills with plastic money, a.k.a. credit cards. They are now the most frequently-used financial product in America, with nearly 170 million Americans holding one, or even multiple cards at once. The nation's credit card debt problem is far from being solved. We still collectively owe nearly $1 trillion to credit card companies, and the average household balance remains too high, at $8,089. Both figures are also likely to rise as the economy reopens from the Coronavirus pandemic. As a result, Americans are projected to increase total credit card debt in 2021 by roughly $50 billion. At 12% interest, the credit card companies will make over $120 billion in 2021 counting late fees, penalties and everything else they add to balances due. Ask yourself – when was the last time you saw a credit card company go out of business? Because they never do.

Investments

Enough negative talk. Let's talk about investing and making money. There are many ways to invest, from coin collecting, the stock market, real estate, baseball cards, and art. I can't tell you where to invest, but I can tell you to find something of value that interests you first then study and learn about it with all your heart. See where your passions lie. Three of the best ways that I know of to make money in America are:

1. Own your own business
2. Invest in the stock market
3. Invest in real estate

I describe having your own business as "prison versus freedom." A person who has never owned a business really doesn't know the perks that come with it. I always try to motivate people to work for themselves and enjoy their freedom. In my opinion, there's no downside to owning your own business, but there are many downsides to working for someone. You can only apply limited skills in a job, but in your own business you can leverage a much greater range of skills. You can apply your full energy and knowledge to create the results output for your clients. There are limited rewards for your best performance on the job, whereas a self-employed person gets a full appreciation for his or her good performance. You build another's credibility in a job, whereas you add to your own reputation and credibility in your own business. You help to reduce the market domination and inflation of the country. You will not have to wait for your paycheck to pay for basic needs.

On the other hand, the stock market is a promising channel for investment income. The average return for the S&P 500 over the past 50 years, adjusted for inflation, is 6.8%. Over the last ten years that return is 11.96%. I love paying attention when I am out and around to the best business to invest in. When my kids were growing up, I spent thousands of dollars on Apple iPods, iPads, and Macbooks. My kids and a lot of their friends had to have the latest gadget that Apple put out, so guess what? I bought Apple stock. It has more than quadrupled in value since I bought it.

Have you ever been to Costco and not seen a line? Usually every cash register is full with six or eight people waiting to check out. How many times have you heard a Costco shopper say, "I just went in to pick up a few things and I ended up spending $300." That's a good business. So guess what I did? I bought Costco stock six years ago for $220 and share. Today, it's worth $450 a share. They were nice enough to send me a $10 dividend for each share of stock I owned at the end of last year. Do you think I love shopping at Costco? You're right—I do. I love owning stocks and learning about how companies grow and change over time.

A year ago my son who works for Garmin in Kansas City, Kansas got a stock option. He called and asked me what he should do. He said most people were cashing them in and buying stuff. I told him that the difference between short-term thinkers and long-term thinkers is their actions. For the people that cashed in and bought something, that money is gone forever. I told him long-term thinkers invest the money and one day he could retire if he so chooses. At the time, the stock was selling for about $83 a share and today it's selling for $156 a share. He is thrilled and has since opened up a brokerage account and is doing real well with his investing.

Investing has changed a lot over the years. I made my first investment in the stock market when I was only thirteen-years old. My grandfather left me $3,000 as part of my inheritance. This was back when you had to look up the stock symbol in the newspaper everyday to see what your stock had done the day before. The dollar amounts were in 1/8th increments just to make it more confusing. Can you imagine what it was like for a thirteen-year old kid trying to figure out what price IBM was selling for at 33 and 5/8th! It's not like today where you have up-to-the-minute information at the tip of your fingers and in dollars on your smartphone.

Technology has made life so much easier than I could have imagined in my childhood. Back then, I used to have to call a stock broker and pay about $100 to place a trade. Today you can buy an unlimited amount of stock in your brokerage account while on-the-go with no brokerage fee. Man, how things have changed over the past fifty years!

Real estate is another great way to make money. It is a very big industry and I predict it will continue growing in the future. Planning to invest in real estate is not a bad idea at all! Cash flow is the primary objective that attracts almost every individual in the real estate industry. Back in 1999 I had sold my starter home for cash, for around $140,000. I was looking for a property to invest in. I asked several realtors around town if they had any good deals. I ended up buying an Advanced Auto Parts building that was already built and being leased back to Advanced Auto Parts. At the time I bought it they were asking $550,000. I told the realtor to offer $525,000, and they came back with a counteroffer of $575,000. As it turns out, the owner wanted to net $550,000 after commissions, so the real estate agent added on a $25,000 commission, and I bought it. Over the years, the interest rate has come down, the rent has gone up, and the value of the property has more than doubled. Today, it's paid for and generates a consistent monthly income. Real estate investment has always been an avenue for wealth and over time real estate investments create equity and cash flow, and hopefully appreciation if well-maintained or in a good location.

As you can see, you can make a million dollars in a lot of different ways and through a number of different vehicles.

My friends and I have discussed our means for financial success and it's always through stocks or real estate. It always amazes me when I have a conversation with someone about investing in the stock market and their first response is, "I don't want to lose money!" That's not what the stock market is for. You will not lose money in the stock market over a long period of time. The stock market is the best way for the average person to make money over the long term.

After my father passed away I decided to teach my kids how to invest. They were all recent college graduates or new to the workforce. In 2016, I opened a brokerage account for each child with $10,000. I told them that the money was theirs for ten years. At the end of ten years, they must return my original $10,000 and they get to keep the balance. Fast forward five years and the accounts have all grown to over $25,000.

It has taught them a valuable lesson about the art of investing. Investing doesn't have to be complicated. In the beginning I started each of the kids with nothing more than the S&P 500 which are the top 500 stocks by size of the stock market. It includes stocks like Apple, Microsoft, Amazon, PayPal, Tesla and Google, and also many old school stocks like Visa, MasterCard, JP Morgan Chase, and even Warren Buffett's company, Berkshire Hathaway. I also purchased $5,000 of the QQQ's which are the top 100 NASDAQ stocks weighted by size. These stocks can be a little more volatile, but over the past five years have outperformed the spiders (S&P 500) two to one. Wall Street brokers try to make things confusing because they don't want you to understand. They want you to feel compelled to rely on them to become financially independent. They want to keep you from learning what it takes to be successful in life. Does this sound familiar? I wonder why schools never taught us any of this.

The Power of Growth

If you have never understood the Eighth Wonder of the World, it's called compound interest. Basically it means that you are making money on the money you've already made. It's almost like free money. Allow me to demonstrate through this question, "Would you rather have a million dollars today or take a penny and double it for 31 days?" Most people choose the million dollars without even thinking. Did you know that if a penny doubled every day for thirty one days will turn into over $10 million dollars? Go ahead and try it. Day 1 – one cent, Day 2 – two cents, Day 3 – four cents, Day 4 – eight cents, Day 5 – sixteen cents, Day 6 – thirty two cents, and after seven days, a whole week, after spending only one quarter of your allotted time you have a whopping 64 cents! How in the world are you going to get to $10 million dollars with only twenty four days left? I'll let you figure that one out, just keep going! On Day 31 you will have $10,737,418.24.

The bottom line is, start investing while you are young in order to take advantage of compound interest. The first thing I would do (if I were starting over) would be to max out my 401(k). Most companies have some sort of a matching plan so for every dollar you invest, they will contribute a certain number of dollars. Who doesn't love free money? I know I do! If that opportunity is not available to you, you can go to any brokerage and start a Roth IRA, which is a special retirement savings account. Some of the more popular brokerages are Fidelity, Schwab, TD Ameritrade, or Vanguard. Most of these brokerages have very low minimums to start investing.

The beauty of a Roth IRA is that you can invest up to $6,000 a year in the account with after-tax money and it grows tax-free until you take it out. The best part is when you take the money out at retirement you don't have to pay any income taxes on it!

Money in Roth IRAs must remain there until you are 59 ½. If it is removed before that there are penalties and interest, so be sure you don't need this money. If you are afraid you might need the money before 59 ½ just open a regular brokerage account so you can access your money anytime. You lose the ability for it to grow tax free, and it's levied with taxes based on your income when you take it out. This is a huge price to pay. Over the years, the government has adjusted the rules from time to time but as of right now it is the best thing available. Just open the account and deposit what you can every year.

Just think: if you put $6,000 a year in a Roth IRA and don't do anything else in thirty years, you will have $180,000 tax free.

There is no guarantee, but the historical average rate of return of the S&P 500 over the last thirty years is 8%. At that rate money will double every ten years. If you start at age twenty with a Roth IRA and invest $6,000 a year for thirty years, at age fifty you will have $1,090,000.

There are all kinds of IRA calculators online and if you play around and plug in different years or interest rates you can see where you will be down the road. When I opened an account for my kids, I told them that I got them to Day 21 with the example of "taking a penny and doubling it for thirty one days." Over the past six years, the accounts are now past Day 22 on their way to Day 23. So they only have to double it eight more times (approximately 56 years) to be worth over $10,000,000 at retirement. If they do this in a Roth IRA and they can withdraw it tax free after age sixty or live in part off of annual distributions and let the remaining balance continue to grow.

◆ ◆ ◆ ◆ ◆

Life is not always sunny. Everyone will have his or her rainy day. With savings in the pocket, a rainy day is just an inconvenience. Without savings, it's a major disaster that could lead to horrible consequences like bankruptcy. If everyone has savings of at least six months to one year of living expenses, the number of people who are struggling to make ends meet would be much smaller. Thus, financial security adds to one's peace of mind because having money in your pocket makes you much better equipped to deal with the challenges that life throws at you.

Chapter 5: Failure Is the ONLY Option!

"One hour per day of study in your chosen field is all it takes. One hour per day of study will put you at the top of your field within three years. Within five years you'll be a national authority. In seven years, you can be one of the best people in the world at what you do." - Earl Nightingale

Now this is a subject I could write an entire book about! Whoever told the tale about success from growing magic beans needs to get their facts right because the pathway to success is never a straight one. Your journey may become tangled with so many twists and turns that you can get lost in the mind maze and lose your purpose. Failure is a word that serves many purposes in our personal growth. Failure is necessary for a successful life. If you go through life trying to avoid failure, then you're not really living a life at all. We all need to take risks and fall flat on our faces, because those are the moments that make us who we are. It allows us to prove to ourselves that we can come back from loss stronger than before.

Failures provide opportunities to understand the gaps between what you wanted and the results you got (internal & external) in any situation. Mind you, gaps always exist. Always. If you're interested at all in getting better results in the future, you will take the opportunity to seek the root causes for the gaps and then adapt your efforts accordingly.

You'll never get to a destination where all conditions are perfectly in your favor and where some or all of those conditions won't change in the next moment. The world always changes around you. You will always fail on some level and must constantly seek to improve. I have failed my way to success. I don't know a single successful person who has become successful without failing many times. Look at Warren Buffett, the greatest investor in the world!

"I made my first investment at age eleven. I was wasting my life up until then." - Warren Buffett

According to a *CNBC* article* published on May 2, 2020:
"Berkshire Hathaway Chairman and billionaire value investor Warren Buffett said that the conglomerate has sold the entirety of its equity position in the U.S. airline industry. The prior stake, worth north of $4 billion in December, included positions in United, American, Southwest and Delta Air Lines.

"As of December, Berkshire owned 42.5 million (10% stake) American shares, 58.9 million (9.2% stake) Delta shares, 51.3 million (10.1% stake) Southwest shares and 21.9 million (7.6% stake) United shares. The stocks are down 62.9%, 58.7%, 45.8% and 69.7%, respectively, in 2020.

* https://www.cnbc.com/2020/05/02/warren-buffett-says-berkshire-sold-its-entire-position-in-airlines-because-of-the-coronavirus.html

"Prior to 2016, Buffett had eschewed airline investments and had been so opposed to putting money into the industry in the past that he told shareholders in a 2007 note that 'if a farsighted capitalist had been present at Kitty Hawk, he would have done his successors a huge favor by shooting Orville down.'"

In an article on *Yahoo News** shared on April 27, 2021, *"Buffett said he'd spent $7 billion to $8 billion amassing stakes in Delta Air Lines, United Airlines, American Airlines and Southwest Airlines. He didn't comment on the exit prices except to say, 'We did not take out anything like $7 [billion] or $8 billion.' This contributed to Berkshire's massive $50 billion loss in the first quarter of 2020. Since then the stocks have taken off, with American and Southwest up over 80% since their May 25, 2020 bottom, while United and Delta are up about 70%. Measuring gains from the May 25, 2020 trough of all four airlines produces even more spectacular results. United was up over 200% over the period, while American was up 190%."*

Enough said! I could probably stop right there, and I think this says volumes about failure! Now here's a ninety-year old guy, the world's greatest investor, who started investing at age eleven, and whose net worth is $109.5 billion as of Memorial Day 2021! And look how badly he screwed up last year.

If you would like to watch a video of failures from another billionaire, Elon Musk and his SpaceX Program are epitomes of that. The number of times they failed in trying to land a booster

* Jared Blikre, "How Warren Buffett's airline stocks have performed since Berkshire Hathaway sold them." posted April 27, 2021 at www.news.yahoo.com

rocket on the ground or on a boat before they finally got it right is pretty surprising, considering that Elon Musk is said to be the best at his job. If you do not believe me, search for "how not to land an orbital rocket booster" on your web browser or go to: https://youtu.be/bvim4rsNHkQ

Rocket boosters used to be discarded in the ocean. Elon thought if rocket boosters could be retrieved and reused, it would save billions of dollars. People told him he was crazy and it wouldn't work, and that he was wasting his time and money. It took years of failure to finally accomplish the task of landing a rocket booster on land and then on a platform in the ocean. But he did it. He failed a thousand times, but he didn't stay that way. He failed his way to success as you will see in the video. I hope you enjoy a good laugh.

My Own Encounters With Failure

I started in a less dramatic fashion, without space rockets or flying saucers. I graduated from Florida State University in the autumn of 1979 without a pot to piss in. Everyone said I should get into sales because I was good with people. I started using two

credit cards that I had managed to acquire in college. The problem with sales, I found out, was because of the high turnover rate, companies preferred to hire those with experience. So how do you get a job in sales if you have no experience? You start at the bottom.

My very first job was with a chemical company, not Dow Chemical, but a father and son conglomerate named Lee Chemical. I was their first employee because their son was starting a new job! That should have told me something right there! This was a small outfit. The father was a retired chemist with Zep Chemicals and was looking for something to do to enhance his retirement. He formulated his own chemicals, bottled them by hand, printed the labels on a copy machine, glued the labels on the bottles with Elmer's glue, boxed them, and out the door they went!

I loaded up the trunk with samples and I was off to conquer the world! This was a commission deal, the more I sold, the more I made. I left no stone unturned. As soon as I hit the road, I could feel myself being charged up with energy. I stopped at every restaurant and hotel in the Florida panhandle. I tried to sell air fresheners, drain cleaner, all-purpose cleaners, window spray, anything at all, you name it.

Talk about hard core sales! Just try to sell a product without a known brand and black and white labels to someone you've never met before. I felt like Michael Keaton playing Ray Kroc in "The Founder" when he was selling milkshake machines before he founded McDonalds. A must-watch if you haven't seen it already! Anyway, after three months of driving five hundred miles a week, maxing out my credit cards, and hardly making enough to feed myself...I FAILED.

Then I got a job at a company called MASCO. My job was selling fundraising opportunities to high school students. I took my briefcase full of samples to sell: candles, knick-knacks, figurines and did a presentation in front of a whole grade. And to motivate the students, we gave away prizes if they hit certain quotas. Beautiful letterman jackets, hats, scarves, monogrammed items, some nice stuff. This was a much larger company that provided a whole week of training to learn scripts and role playing, and to become familiar with their products. Basically, their way of doing things! With failures come many lessons. The first lesson is *experience*. When we go through something, we acquire and can walk away with firsthand experience. This helps us develop a deeper understanding of life. The experience of failing at something is quite valuable. It completely transforms our frame-of-mind through the induction of pain. It makes us reflect on the nature of things to transform and improve our future selves. But wait for it… because I haven't yet failed in this story.

I started right after New Year's Day in 1980. I was so broke I had to borrow airfare from my parents just to fly home for Christmas. I'll never forget the sick feeling of not being able to afford a single Christmas present. I was so excited to get started on the first day of January after returning to Tallahassee. Off I went again, high school to high school, burning up gas, still on commission with three of my roommates' credit cards, since mine were maxed out at a whopping $1,000 limit. Talk about faith, friendship, and someone believing in you!

This company believed in incentives and most of the new salespeople were just starting their careers. The prize package was incredible. It was twelve items somebody starting out in life could use. A 13" color TV, a microwave, a set of luggage, a silver tea set, a 12-place setting of china, a leather traveling suit bag, a toaster oven, and various other items along those lines. I had mild success, sold a few classes, and enjoyed working with the kids but the problem was you don't get paid until the program is over. I didn't think about it when I started working but the kids go home for the summer! I made a few bucks, enjoyed the work, gained some confidence in myself, but didn't have the money to go a whole summer with no cash flow. The good news is, even though I didn't come anywhere close to the quota to win those fabulous prizes, the company either felt sorry for me or they got my address mixed up with someone who did win the prize package. Once every week for the next twelve weeks, a package arrived with one of those prizes. I didn't ask any questions...but I failed!

When we moved into a new house in 2019, I still had that silver tea set, now tarnished and old-looking. In the move, my wife took it to Goodwill to de-clutter. When I asked her what happened, she told me I had forty years to do something with that tea set. I looked on eBay and saw it was worth about $1,500 cleaned up. Oh well, I was never much of a tea drinker anyway.

Then the next job I found was selling motivational seminars through the local Chamber of Commerce to their members. Basically what I was supposed to do was to call the individual members, talk to them, and maybe play a recording of a motivational speaker that would come to town and talk about different topics like time management, hiring personnel, and various other subjects that would help the members. I did my song-and-dance and sold tickets for however many people in their organization wanted to attend. Same old story. Unfortunately, like my two previous jobs it involved running up and down the highways, visiting different cities, and getting deeper in the hole with my credit cards. I continued working for this company for several months but ended up spending about twenty nights a month in a hotel sharing a room with a chain-smoking seasoned veteran salesperson. I would come home every other week to cut the grass, check my mail, and put the bills I couldn't pay into a neat pile.

Finding a New Path

After several months of this lifestyle and looking at the salespeople I worked with who had been doing these types of sales their whole lives, I could tell this was not my cup of tea either. I failed. It was about this time that I decided to make a change and head to Charleston and Raleigh during my two-week vacation to seek employment. Here, failure taught me another lesson about *personal growth*. When we stumble and fall, we grow and mature as human beings. We reach a deeper understanding about our lives and why we're doing the things that we're doing. We reflect and take things into perspective, developing meaning from painful situations.

It took a couple of years to get back on my feet, pay off my roommates and my credit cards, and get a few dollars in the bank for a cushion to live on. When I started working for my business partner in the video game business, he asked me what I wanted in life. I told him I wanted to be self-employed because I was only worth what a route man got paid, and I wanted to be an owner.

He said, "Go find a business to put video games in. I'll put up the money and we'll split the profits." Within a week I had found a location, and my partner Hampton Metts came into town and wrote a check for $48,000 to purchase the inventory in the convenience store.

We were all excited about starting our new business venture and just before Hampton left, he asked me how much money I

Craig at Socastee Deli Video Games shop

had saved up at the time. I told him $7,800 was all I had to my name, and he said, "Before I leave, write me a check for $7,800." At first, I thought he was kidding but unfortunately, he wasn't. He said, "Now that we are partners, you owe me half of the $48,000 or $24,000, and after this check you will only owe me $16,200. I know you'll be here when I come back from my vacation in the Bahamas." Here I was, back to square one again. Fortunately, the business was very profitable and I was able to pay him back in seventeen weeks. This event made me learn the value of things. When thinking about your past failures, think about how much value you brought to the table. One of the grandest lessons that we can learn from all the failures we face in life is the necessity to create and spread an exceedingly high amount of value. I did not bring much to the table, but I learned fast enough.

Fast forward a few years. I was finally getting ahead and decided to invest in the stock market. I went to my banker and informed him about how I was thinking about selling a piece of property I owned and putting the money in the stock market. This was in 1998, just prior to the internet bubble. He said, "I got a better idea. Why don't I lend you the money using the property as collateral, then if you make money, you will have the property and the profits, and if you lose money, you can sell the property and pay off the loan." I said it sounds good and I borrowed $150,000. Between 1998 and when the market crashed in 2000, I was riding the internet wave. In three years, by taking large risks I had increased my portfolio balance to $1.5 million dollars. Life was good. I was living way below my means in a 1,500 square foot house. The business was going well, and I had purchased several pieces of real estate along the way… and then the dot.com crash happened.

My $1.5 million dollars became $500,000 in less than six months before I finally cashed out because I could not take any more pain. When you start with $150,000 and increase it tenfold in three years and then lose two thirds of it in less than six months it may be a win, but it sure felt like I failed. Here, failure taught me to be resilient in the face of calamity. When we fail in life, the circumstances demand that we develop resilience. The more times we fail, the more resilient we become. And it is imperative on the path to acquiring great success to familiarize ourselves with resilience. Because if we think that we're going to make waves on the first attempt, or even the first few tries, then we're sure to set ourselves up for a far more painful failure. Resilience aids success by setting the stage to win. Resilience brings the expectations that true success will take an enormous amount of work and effort.

Three months after the stock market crashed in March 2000, video poker was outlawed in South Carolina on June 30th. Video poker was the main source of my income. So, there I was, forty-two years old with no apparent source of income, and I had just lost one million dollars on paper. I had greatly increased

my overhead in opening another store, hiring more employees, then having to pay close to $20,000 in property taxes. By now I was married with four kids and my monthly expenses had increased dramatically. It was scramble time. Over the next four years I got involved in the sun-tanning business... I failed. The pawn store business... I failed. The video tape rental business... I failed (thank you, Blockbuster and Netflix).

During that time I still owned close to two hundred video poker machines. We ventured into Alabama and Texas. Over the next three years, we opened eight arcades, and for one reason or another, we had to close them all. In one circumstance, my partner and I purchased a building in Birmingham, Alabama on Center Point Parkway. After spending $150,000 converting the building into an arcade, the county decided that too many arcades were opening and put a moratorium on new licenses. We never even got started or opened that arcade. Talk about bad timing!

We went all the way to South Padre Island in the tip of Texas, 1,500 miles from home, and partnered with a local businessman to open an arcade. After spending a month getting them set up, I drove home to Myrtle Beach and turned on the television. The ticker tape across the bottom of the screen said "Barge hits bridge going to South Padre Island at roughly 2:00 a.m., while cars disappeared over the edge not realizing what had happened. Three 80-foot sections collapsed, killing eight and three survived." This was only four days after September 11th, 2001. It was a disaster. Watching the message at the bottom of the screen made me feel like I was in a nightmare. Not only was this devastating, but when you have one hundred fifty machines on an island with no bridge you are out of business... I failed. This time I had nothing at all to say because nobody can contain calamity. Failure at this point taught me how all of us human beings are helpless and incapacitated in the face of hardship sent by the Universe. Nevertheless, there is always hope for a better tomorrow.

With my accumulated funds running low, I decided to get into the unbelievably hot real estate market in 2006. Using most of the money, I decided to buy two ocean-front condos. Properties were in such high demand that a person had to get on a waiting list to purchase a unit. This deal was a quick flip to make some money to replenish my reserves. I paid $225,000 for each unit with a 20% down payment. The monthly mortgage was a little over $1,800 and the HOA fees were $1,200 per month. Each unit grossed about $20,000 per year, of which I got 55% before expenses and upkeep. You can do the math on this, but I was losing about $20,000 per year for twelve years. I sold one condo for $85,000 in March 2018, and the other I sold for $89,000 with owner financing in April 2018. There is nothing worse than being trapped in a real estate deal when you don't have the money to pay it off and must continue making payments until you come up with the money, or pay the mortgage down to the point you can afford to take a loss...I failed. Yet again.

I, like Elon Musk and Warren Buffett, have failed my way to success by making mistakes, learning from them, regrouping, starting over, and trying something else. The beautiful thing about life is that there were many more failures than successes, but because of all of the things I learned through my failures I was able to have greater successes. Over the years, working in different business and making a variety investments have given me the ability to be successful, happy, and financially independent. I hope I have proven to you in this chapter that no matter how big you are or if you are just beginning in life, failing is not negative. It is a way to learn, grow, and become successful. That is why failure is the only option.

Failure provides many life lessons. First and foremost, failure teaches us to estimate our powers realistically. Long-term success can lead to the naïve belief that you will be always at the top of your game. This deceptive belief can prevent further growth and development. Someone engaged in this euphoric mindset may believe that they are sufficiently equipped to thrive continually. Your strength can be overestimated, or even start to degrade. This kind of mindset doesn't help with facing current realities. It's easy to lose control over a situation. As a result, a failure is unavoidable. But failure is not the only negative side of overconfidence.

The basic message of a failure is that something has gone wrong and needs to be made right. It's a necessary push to reassess abilities. It's a call to determine what measures have to be taken. Failures stimulate us to find solutions. Overcoming obstacles trains you to cope with difficulties of any kind. Failure demands new conclusions and changes of direction. When you get knocked out, failure teaches a person to analyze cause and effect. Crucial issues can be invisible until disaster strikes. Once you become aware that there are problems, they can't be ignored. It's time to embrace a new perspective.

Failure is a powerful instrument for self-improvement if used properly. We should not see it as a total loss but an invaluable life lesson. In this case it opens new possibilities and visions that can help a person rise to higher heights than before.

The first landlord I dealt with in the arcade business came by the store one day and I was complaining about everything that was going wrong - the employees, vendors, customers, and various other things. He was a tobacco-chewing old boy who had retired from the Air Force. He gave me great words of wisdom that I live by today. He said, "Craig, when you are in business for yourself, you just got to get excited about what's going to go wrong next," as he spat a big wad of chewing tobacco in my parking lot. I didn't shout at him for doing that because of the wisdom he had given me that day.

Chapter 6: Balance Is the Key to a Happy Life

"Life is about growth and exploration, not achieving a fixed state of balance. You have a very limited time on Earth to experience all that you can. Figuring out how to squeeze the most out of your family, work, and spirituality is your life's purpose. Go do it." - Mel Robbins

Now comes the tricky part! You have goals, a plan, and a timeframe. You're excited to see your plan become a reality. You're all charged up to take the reins of your life in your own hands. Let me tell you how much I love the energized spirit people gain when they've made the decision to take over the world and change the entire course of their life for good. Oh, the sweet smell of success lingering in the air! You're all set, well-prepared, ready to start your own business, drive that new Corvette, get that big diamond ring, and explore every nook and cranny of the world.

But why do people focus so often on material things and believe that a new car or a house by the ocean would bring the happiness that we so desperately desire? Or that a Prada bag or a pair of Christian Louboutin shoes are the secret to happiness? Let me tell you what I've learned from my years of experience: the key to a truly happy life is **balance**.

Perhaps spirituality has taken a backseat in your life. Out of the many goals you've set, in my opinion, your spiritual goals are the most important. If you truly don't know where you're going, you are *not* going to like your final destination. I digress, I'm saving that for the last chapter. Surely you have a career, mortgage, partner, friends, activities... and most certainly you have a life. There are multiple dimensions of life, and it is entirely within your purview to keep all those dimensions in balance. If you place your total focus on a single aspect of life while neglecting all the others, there will be unattractive consequences.

Consider Different Areas of Life

Your goals should encompass a wide range of life's dimensions. For example, don't direct your entire focus and energy toward your career; it's important to integrate time for social life as well. Set a weekly goal of going on a date night with your spouse, and strive for a variety of different dating activities. If you want to make huge strides in your most intimate relationship, choose a day every month to make a romantic gesture like sending flowers, a card that says nothing more than "I love you," or some other thoughtful gift. These small gestures have a huge impact, so let them do their magic.

When it comes to taking care of our bodies, we could probably all do better. Our body is like a temple and must be treated like one. Once I was talking about health and fitness with a friend who is a tri-athlete. He asked, "When you were sixteen years old, if you could pick any car you wanted with one caveat: that car would be the only car you would own for the rest of your life. How would you treat it? How often would you take it in for a tune up, or an oil change? Would you feed it cheap gas and oil or give it the best? Would you leave it out in the sun all day to fade and rust? Of course not, right? Well, that's how you should think about your body!"

Ask yourself the following questions. Are you feeding your body good food or junk food because it's more convenient? Are you getting regular checkups? Are you going to the gym three times a week? You only get one body so be sure to take care of it. Sure, prosthetics are making waves in the world, but c'mon, nothing beats the original. Cancer is a dangerous, lethal disease and its rise has only surged over time. I think a large part of the problem we have with cancer and obesity in this country is largely because of the invention of fast food and processed foods during the 1950s. There is a great documentary on Netflix called "What the Health." I watched it and convinced many of my friends to watch it as well. Watching it changed my life and the lives of several of my friends for the better. I challenge you and everyone around you to watch "What the Health" if you are at all concerned about your health.

Developing a successful career is a central life facet for most people. I spent the last seventeen years of my life in the real estate business. My mentor in the business told me that real estate brings out the best and the worst in people. There are the housewives that hope to make one sale a year and the aggressive young entrepreneurs who have billboards all over town. They kill themselves for that one sale that would turn their life around.

If there is one area of life where people experience the biggest challenges with balance in their lives, it's their jobs or business. Why? Creating and sustaining a source of income is rarely optional. We have to do it no matter what happens. I know it very well because it happened to me. If the boss is paying you to show up, you show up! If you have your own business, but you don't show up, you're out of business.

One of my early-life goals was to create enough passive income through real estate, stocks, and business to support my lifestyle without getting out of bed. I wanted nothing less than total freedom. If I wanted to golf all day, I could do it. If I wanted to sit on the beach and drink margaritas, I could do it. If I wanted to go to the movies and eat that big tub of fresh popcorn, I could do it. And in a sort of cruel way, if I wanted to get up early and sit on the front porch in my pajamas and wave to the neighbors going to work, I would do that, and then still be there on the front porch to welcome them home after a hard day at work!

I worked my butt off for seven days a week, 365 days a year, sometimes twenty-four hours solid because I wanted freedom in a free country! I figured it would take a net worth of $3-4 million consisting of investments, real estate, and passive income to be in that position. By the age of forty-two, I was there! My business was booming, I had generated multiple sources of revenue like income-producing real estate, a million and a half in the stock market, and lots of assets! Life was going great. I was having fun. The world was my oyster and I was achieving my desires. I enjoyed what I was doing, plus I had good people working for me, so I had flexibility. I went golfing, I went to the matinee. The way I see it now, my money was working for me, and I wasn't working for it anymore...*I was free!*

But like they say, nothing good lasts forever. My time of blossoming was cut short. As I wrote in Chapter 5, my arcade business got into trouble, my investments tanked, and boom, my sources of income went down the drain!

In retrospect, I think it was God's way of saying, *slow down cowboy, hold your horses! You're getting way ahead of yourself, and your priorities are all messed up.* I'm sharing more details about my story because I truly want you to understand that no matter how well you think you have your life figured and planned out, it's amazing how quickly it can all turn on a dime. In less than six months, two legs of my three-legged stool had been kicked out from underneath me. I was forty-two with a brand-new house, a wife and four kids, and with all that comes lots of overhead. And in case you can't figure it out, a big overhead, a declining net worth, and a negative cash flow does not make for a very happy life.

It was time to start over, again. Life was a little more complicated at this point. I wasn't alone anymore; I now had a family to
care for. My life went from being on top of the world to sheer
chaos. During the twenty years from ages twenty-two and forty-
two, I was laser focused on achieving my freedom. As a result, the
rest of my life was way out of balance. I didn't have much of a
spiritual life. I had indulged in the good things in life like my bi-
annual trips to Las Vegas. I wasn't taking care of my health and
had ballooned to over 300 pounds. I got out of breath walking out
to get the mail. Oh sure, I had all the toys and the trappings of
success, an airplane, a Mercedes, a brand new 4,000 square-foot
house on the golf course, and even a hot tub in the backyard. I can
distinctly remember calling my wife at home while I was setting
up the arcade in Brownsville, Texas on South Padre Island. One of
our children was screaming in the background and my wife was
crying on the phone saying, "You have to do something. I can't
take this anymore."

I was 1,500 miles away chasing my dreams. What could I do?
I called some friends and asked them if they could go over to my
house and take my son for a couple hours to give my wife some
relief. That seemed like the only plausible option to me back then,
but now that I look at it, it all seems extremely unfair. I am going
to talk about how important faith and friends are in upcoming
chapters, but for right now, let me just say if we didn't have good
friends, I might not be married anymore.

You must be wondering by now how one can ensure balance. To give you some more ideas to implement, here is a list of nine items that might free up some time and create the opportunity for a well-balanced life.

1. **No Electronics Day:** It's amazing to see how people, both young and old, are tethered to their cell phones. Pick a day and plan to do something with the family that does not involve electronics. You will be amazed at how much better you feel. You will find out that the world can carry on without you for one day.

2. **Don't be afraid to say "NO."** I thought that being in the real estate business meant that I could control my own time. Unfortunately, all my clients thought that I worked all day and all night. Being a people pleaser, I would always try to help. One of the enigmas in real estate is that the small deals often take more time than the big deals. At a seminar I attended, the speaker asked, "When was the last time you turned down a listing?" I was shocked because that made no sense to me. Why would you turn down a listing? He explained that if you spend your time finding good listings and leaving the small listings for somebody else, you have a much more enjoyable life. I did this and it felt like the chains came off. At the time I had over 100 listings. Do you think my life was in balance?

3. **Minimize the negative people around you.** We have enough negative things bombarding us every day like the Coronavirus, riots in the street, murders, and hatred. Much of this

negative stuff hitting you from all angles can't be controlled. So, for God's sake, why on earth would you hang around negative people when that's something you can control? Surround yourself with people who are going somewhere, successful people, and people with positive attitudes.

4. **Make time for you.** This is probably the hardest thing to do for the typical overworked and overwhelmed person. When was the last time you just laid in the grass and stared at the sky trying to pick out images in the clouds? If you are outdoorsy, take a camping trip by yourself and look at the stars. Give yourself time to reflect and relax.

5. **Set aside quality time with your family and friends.** On the first day of each month, mark off days on your calendar to spend time with your immediate family and with friends. Go with friends to local festivals. Enjoy and get to know the people around you. When was the last time someone asked you, "what would you like to do today?" You have my undivided attention. Leave the cell phone and watch in the car so you are not distracted by emails, texts, and time.

6. **Pay it forward.** When I go through a drive-thru, I ask the cashier how much the person's order behind me in line costs and then pay for it. You will be amazed as people pull up to pay and the cashier tells them it has already been taken care of. The looks of bewilderment in their eyes is inspiring.

7. **Don't get in a rut.** We travel the same roads to work or to go home. Mix it up a little bit by taking a different route just to

see what's going on in your environment. Find a new mom-and-pop restaurant and support local businesses. We all seem to have our five or six go-to restaurants. Why not expand that number to twenty?

8. **Expand your comfort zone.** Take a dance class, sign up for a course on air-conditioner repair at the local college, rent a kayak, or a stand-up paddleboard for the day. Find something that you want to know more about and team up with the people who can help you experience it.

9. **Be thankful for what you have.** Constantly be on the lookout for the good things in life. Friends, family, health, a roof over your head, the car you drive…anything that helps you appreciate life. You will find that when you start searching for things to be thankful for, more and more reasons for gratitude will be revealed to you.

Balance is subjective, which means that you decide what life-balance works for you. A person who lives their life in a balanced manner pays attention to their basic physical needs first. The things usually taken to excess are eating, drinking, lack of sleep, and a lack of regular exercise. Once those are taken into account, you have a good basis for deciding on what life-balance works for you personally.

If you feel that you are on autopilot most of the time you are probably reacting to your life instead of acting in it. Take some time at the end of every day to evaluate what you actually did

82

that day and why you did it. If something significant occurred, how did you react? Did you react without thinking, allowing your subconscious to take control at that moment? Spending time in reflection can reveal areas of your life that feel unbalanced. How can you purposely change anything in those parts? Introspection is a valuable tool for learning about yourself.

The better you know yourself, the less time you'll waste chasing rainbows that are the wrong color for you. Self-knowledge requires thoughtful living. Evaluating your current position in life and considering the steps you took to get there is an encyclopedic source of useful information. People find that journaling and meditation are helpful methods for gaining self-knowledge. At the end of the day, gaining self-knowledge will help you sustain and maintain your balance.

I hope this makes you aware of how easy it is for life to become out of balance. It takes constant attention, like the guy that spins the plates on top of the cue sticks. One day you will find yourself with a well-balanced plate with good speed and no issues. Then you look down at the other plates and a couple of them are starting to wobble, so you have to get those plates spinning again. Don't worry if a plate drops every now and then. Review the state of balance in your different areas of life and work to keep your plates spinning properly.

Chapter 7: Where's Your Bucket List?

"Twenty years from now you will be more disappointed by the things you didn't do than by the ones you did do. So, throw off the bowlines, sail away from the safe harbor. Catch the trade winds in your sails. Explore. Dream. Discover."
- Mark Twain

The above quote by Mark Twain identifies a truth that exists in people's lives. We're all so busy making a living that we forget how to live. We forget that our work is just a part of our life, it is not our whole life. Being preoccupied with keeping up with Joneses makes us forget our purpose. We lose track of what drives us, what makes us happy. We stop searching for the very thing that makes life worth living.

There is nothing wrong with working, but work is something that you should be passionate about. We grow up hearing about how being rich and successful is all that matters, so that is what we strive for. We get lost in the day-to-day rat race of life where people are competing against each other. Most people can't even recall what gives them joy because we've been conditioned to believe that joy exists in living up to society's expectations.

Why do people stay in a job that doesn't put them on a path for success? There are plenty of reasons, but these are some of the most common:

1. **Obligations**: The main motivation for individuals going to work on a day-to-day basis is to meet their obligations to pay the bills. It could be kids, a home loan, or something else.

2. **The Dread of Being Wrong:** Many individuals worry that the choices they make aren't right. They feel that something might go wrong, or they will fall flat on their face before they've even begun. Worry prevents them from attempting to find a different way to make a living. It's easier to keep doing what they're doing instead of searching for something better.

3. **Fear:** People are afraid to change because of the unknown. They talk themselves out of change before they even get started. Change might require moving to a different place, an unknown new boss and co-workers, with the additional fear of having insufficient funds to survive until the new job begins.

So how can you find purpose in your life? Do you have a bucket list of all the things that you want to do in life that will make YOU happy? Are you ready for some fun? This is where you get to experience the rewards after all the goal setting, tracking your progress, delaying gratification, and working hard to achieve your goals!

But what exactly is a bucket list? How do you even set one up? What should be on it? How long should the list be? All great questions.

Simply put, a bucket list is a set of experiences that someone wants to have before they "kick the bucket."

That's a little morbid but that's what it is. People are great procrastinators. It's a little like preparing a Will. I'll get to it one day; I'll take that trip one day; I'll go to a Super Bowl one day. But it never seems to happen!

The items on your bucket list have to motivate you! If you get seasick, I wouldn't put a cruise on the top of my list! Figure out what you are passionate about and write down your ideas.

Some people love to travel so their bucket list should be heavily weighted in that direction. Travel has become a lot less fun with lockdowns, Covid, cancellations, and delays. If traveling appeals to you, take this into consideration and book trips with fewer destinations and longer stays so if you encounter delays it won't mess up your whole trip.

How long should your bucket list be? It should be long enough to always give you an adventure to look forward, but not such a huge list that it becomes overwhelming. This will depend on free time and cash flow. Cash flow is a major determinant in the length of your bucket list and what you can or cannot afford to do. Even if you don't have the money to fund your bucket list at the present time, there is nothing wrong with dreaming. There is no age limit to when you can achieve what you want to. Here are some fun ideas that friends and family have done.

I have a nephew who loves football. He and a friend have "see a game in every major college football stadium in the country" on their bucket list. They're almost halfway done with this goal.

I have an aunt and uncle who are approaching age ninety. They retired at sixty and never looked back! They love traveling and hit the road shortly after they retired. Over the past thirty years they have been to 248 countries and been on 50+ cruises! One cruise lasted for five months. How's that for a bucket list? When they got too old physically for taking those big trips, they jumped in their Cadillac and took mini-vacations to visit friends. Their goal was to visit every state capital...which they did. It's not my cup of tea, but whatever floats your boat.

Several years ago one of my bucket list items was the "illusive trip around the country." I was between jobs and school was almost out for the summer so we started planning the trip. The day the kids got out of school, we loaded up the conversion van and

headed west to see this big, beautiful country we live in. It was the trip of a lifetime. We traveled for five weeks, went 7,257 miles and crossed twenty-five states. We saw the Grand Canyon, Mount Rushmore, the Grand Tetons, Yellowstone, and Zion National Park. We took a side trip to Las Vegas, the Coral Pink Sands Dunes State Park, and finished up at Cedar Point in Ohio. I highly recommend this trip to anyone who has the time and the money to do so.

To get started, create a short-term list, a medium-term list, and a long-term list. This is a dynamic, not static, list. What turns you on this year might be completely different next year. Here are twenty questions to get you started:

1. What is the one country in the world you would like to visit?

2. If you had one month to live, what would you do?

3. What types of exotic foods do you want to try?

4. What's a terrifying idea that you would like to overcome?

5. Are there any activities or sports that you want to attend in person?

6. What concerts do you want to attend?

7. What has always been your biggest dream in life?

8. What classes have you always thought about taking?

9. If money and fear were not an issue what would you do?

10. What celebrity have you always wanted to meet in person?

11. What trip would you like to do with family and friends?

12. In what ways do you want to improve yourself physically, mentally or spiritually?

13. What skills do you want to acquire?

14. Is there a charity you have always wanted to support?

15. What was your childhood dream — is it still relevant today?

16. If you won a multi-million dollar lottery today, what would you do?

17. If you were on your deathbed, what would be your regrets?

18. What travel stories would you want to share with your grand-children?

19. If you had three wishes what would they be?

20. Is there someplace you have always wanted to take your spouse, best friend, or parents?

This should give you some good ideas on where to start your own bucket list. Have fun, be challenged, and get started today! Be sure to include big items as well as smaller ones so as you accomplish your goals you can reward yourself by doing something on your bucket list. Good luck and have fun!

Chapter 8: Choose Your Friends Wisely

"Friendship is the hardest thing in the world to explain. It's not something you learn in school. But if you haven't learned the meaning of friendship, you really haven't learned anything."
— Muhammad Ali

People are good. In fact, I need to go way beyond that statement. People are unbelievable—they are kind, generous, caring, compassionate, loving, giving, and fun.

A good friend of mine and a neighbor who lived three doors down from us was diagnosed with ALS about six months before I was. He told me one of the greatest things about this disease is that you'll be amazed at how many people will come forward and tell you how much of an influence you have had in their lives. I had no idea what he was talking about.

Boy, do I understand now. I could write a book about how right he was. I am going to share a couple of examples.

A year ago, I received a beautiful handmade inspirational card in the mail one day with a return address that I didn't recognize. I asked my wife if she knew who it was. She wasn't sure either but thought it might be the couple that sits behind us in church. I said, "But we don't even know them except when the preacher says turn and greet your neighbor." Upon further investigation it turned out it was them. I did a little stalking to find out more about them and discovered he was a Navy Seal. I sent his wife a message and said, "Certainly you must have better things to do than make these beautiful cards for someone you hardly know." I told her that she must be a pretty special person. We invited them over for a porch visit and pizza, nothing fancy, just a casual get together. It turns out I was correct in my assessment. They came by at 7:00 and when we stopped talking for long enough to look at our watches it was 11:30. Friends. Choose them wisely. To give you a better idea of how special this couple is in addition to the baked goods I have received, she has sent me a handmade card every week for almost a year.

About six months ago my college roommate came to visit me in Myrtle Beach. We started talking about the good old days and how this might be my last chance to have a homecoming. We thought it might be fun to invite some of our fraternity brothers to

have a homecoming at my house in Myrtle Beach. It's been forty-five years since I started college in 1976. The fraternity has since been kicked off campus and the fraternity house closed down in 2017. It took some detective work and a call to the national headquarters in Charlotte to try and find addresses, emails, and phone numbers. The response was incredible. Of the twenty-two brothers we tried to contact, thirteen brothers and six wives attended the homecoming reunion. Now that's friendship! They came from Los Angeles, Phoenix, St. Louis, Fort Lauderdale, Fort Walton Beach, and various other cities. We had a great time and I gave each of them a USB drive with over 800 photos from our years in college. We started showing them the pictures on my TV at 8 pm. I did not want it to get boring, so around 9 pm I asked if they wanted to stop. They emphatically said no, and the slide show ended after midnight. Friends. It's been forty years since I had seen most of my fraternity brothers. That's what good friends are all about.

◆◆◆◆◆

Would you like to know where you will be five years from now? You can easily know where you'll be, what you'll be doing, and what your income level will be. If you want to know how, the answer is simple: by assessing the friends you've chosen.

The phrase "A man is known by the company he keeps" comes from Aesop (620-564 B.C.E.). The fable is called *The Ass and his Purchaser*. "A man wished to purchase an ass, and agreed with its owner that he should try out the animal before he bought him. He took the ass home and put him in the straw yard with his other asses, upon which the new animal left all the others and at once joined the one that was most idle and the biggest eater of them all. Seeing this, the man put a halter on him and led him back to his owner. On being asked how, in so short a time, he could have made a trial of him, he answered, "I do not need a trial; I know that he will be just the same as the one he chose for his companion."*

An individual is like people in whom he invests his time and energy, and they will share similar personal and moral principles. An individual typically connects with people who are similar. The friends you associate with enjoy going to the same places and doing the same activities.

If you want to change your life, choose the type of friend you want to be like. Here are some secrets to doing so:

1. **Associate higher.** Ever since I was a little boy, I always wondered why some people seemed to be so much more successful than others. When I was ten years old I wanted to get a motorcycle. Obviously I was too young. My best friend was my 5th grade teacher because he had a motorcycle, a Yamaha 180, and he kept it at our house because he lived in an apartment two blocks away. He was having trouble with people stealing parts off of it at his apartment complex. I drove it all

* https://aesopsfables.org/F11_The-Ass-and-His-Purchaser.html

over town with no license and no helmet. How's that for asso-
ciating with someone in a higher position than you are? If you
are focused on taking your life, career, or business to the next
level, then why not associate with people on that next level
up? Doing this will help expand your mind to greater possibilities. It is natural to feel most comfortable with people who
are like you, and that's OK. However, it's good to step outside
of your comfort zone and spend time with friends who can
expose you to greater things, new information, and a higher
level of living. If you value these friendships, you will soon
find yourself advancing too.

2. **Choose friends that you can trust.** The easiest way I have
found to tell if somebody is a real friend is to lend them
money. Over the years I have let people borrow $100,000,
$50,000, $10,000, and other smaller amounts. Before I lend
friends money, I always ask myself: if I don't get paid back
will it affect our friendship? So far in my life I have only had
one person not pay me back in full. Sometimes it took longer
for people to pay me back than originally planned, but eventually they all made good. Lending money is a good way to
find out who your friends really are, but you better be prepared not to be paid back. If this puts you in a financial bind,
then I would not recommend doing it.

3. **Choose friends with common goals.** When I see somebody
who is doing something that I would like to do, I have no
problem approaching them and asking them if they would
like to be a partner. Depending on the situation, I try to let

94

them know my strengths and how I can be a benefit to them with whatever projects the partnership entails. When you have friends with common goals, particularly as an entrepreneur, you can motivate each other. You can work on your goals together and encourage each other in reaching them.

4. **Choose friends who can bring balance in areas where you are weaker**. I have always admired those people that seem to have a beautiful balance in life between work, vacations, family, and spirituality. I rarely take a vacation because it seems like there's always one more thing to do. We all have our strengths and weaknesses -- you know what yours are. With the right friends, you can tap into the way they plan and organize their life based on their beliefs about what's really important in life. Maybe you aren't the best at identifying the priorities in your life, but if you have a friend who can help you identify what's important, enlist their help! When you utilize each other's strengths, everyone wins.

5. **Choose friends who stretch, motivate, and encourage you**. Have you ever had a friend who just makes you feel drained when they leave? The person says negative things about other people, he doesn't add much to a conversation, and he doesn't really inspire or challenge you. No one wants a friend who is negative or down all the time. It's usually the people who are uplifting and positive that we naturally want to be around. Which category do your friends fall into? What do your conversations with them sound like? The best types of friends

will be there to offer a listening ear and help you put a positive spin on any situation.

6. **Choose friends who share the same interests.** I have a lot of different interests, from flying to sports to business and the stock market. I find that I have a completely different set of friends for each of these activities that I enjoy. Friends with similar interests make life more fun. You can enjoy outings and activities together. When you have shared interests, you can get out and do things together.

7. **Choose friends who have a thirst for knowledge.** Life is about learning, growing, and advancing. With friends like this, you can learn from each other. It's always great to have a friend who can recommend a good book or share information with you to help you on your path. Friends who are avid readers are usually great conversationalists and fun to talk to as well.

8. **Choose friends who are doing things you would like to do.** During the real estate crash, I had a client who was buying, fixing up, and then flipping properties. I asked him if he was looking for a partner and he said no. While we were working together, he found out how valuable I was because I could get access to houses in foreclosure, access to the MLS, a good work ethic, and a lot of experience in construction. I made myself so valuable that we ended up doing twenty-seven flips together and we made money on every one of them. A good partner can help you stay accountable and ensure follow

through. Allow them to check in on you and ask you about your progress, and do the same for them.

9. **Choose friends who will celebrate your success**. It is very hard to find someone who is truly happy for your success. Friendships can impact your future and career. Find friends who celebrate you, not just tolerate you. A true friend will celebrate every milestone, accomplishment, and success story on your journey. They will be genuinely happy to see you succeed and be the first to say "congratulations!" Friends like this can be rare, so when you find them keep them close!

10. **Choose friends who are "Git 'Er Done" people**. The one thing in the real estate business that lets you partner up with git 'er done people is the time value of money. Every day the interest clock is ticking and eating into your profits. It forces you to "git 'er done" or you'll watch the bank soak up all of your hard work. Git 'er done people are serious about their goals and serious about success. They don't treat life casually or waste time on frivolous pursuits. They take fast action and get things done. If you consider yourself a git 'er done person, it's important that you have friends who operate the same way.

11. **Give what you expect to get.** Our dearest and oldest friends in Myrtle Beach are these kinds of people, except they always seem to give more than we give them in return. If you want a real challenge, hang around givers and then try to out-give them. This is an awesome kind of friendship and you never know what to expect. A few examples of what this couple has

done include traveling from Myrtle Beach to Ohio to attend my mother's funeral. They quietly planted flowers in the flower bed of our new home when I was unable to because of my health. They've also joined us for every New Year's Eve for the past twenty-one years.

Every friendship is a give-and-take. If you expect great friends, you first must be one yourself. If you live by the Golden Rule of treating others **better** than you would want to be treated, then you won't be disappointed -- you will find your friendships fulfilling and rewarding.

If you want to do all or many of the things listed above for someone you care about, you already know how to be a good friend. Choose friends who are dependable and honest. Choose friends you are proud to know, people you admire, who show you love and respect — people who reciprocate kindness. Take some time to evaluate your relationships. Do your friends meet the criteria given above? Can you call any of them your partners? If so, then great! If not, then it's time to branch out and start establishing some new relationships. Continue gradually into new friendships until you discover shared qualities and viewpoints. A significant attribute of an effective friendship is knowing you can depend on your friend to be there to help you, invest energy with you, and be straightforward with you. With the secrets above, you can boost the quality of your relationships and your long-term success.

Chapter 9: The Secret of Living Is Giving

"At the end it's not about what you have or even what you've accomplished. It's about who you've lifted up, who you've made better. It's about what you've given back."
- Denzel Washington

This is where the fun begins and life really gains the purpose, fulfillment, and joy that comes with giving. You've set your goals, you've worked hard, and you're at the point in life where you are making more money than you are spending. You're accumulating money, your money is making money and you feel really good about life. Now, you want to give back. There is no better feeling than surprising someone with a gift, lending money to a friend in need, donating to charity, or giving anonymously. I'll give you a few stories of some of the things I've been able to do that have brought me great joy in life. This is not to brag, but to show you examples of the joy of giving.

The most recent example as I stated earlier in the book was my 63rd drive-by birthday party where we raised $7,500 for the South Carolina ALS Association, but I've already talked about that in Chapter 2. I won't repeat myself, however, I do want to thank my wife for putting it together; it was a huge success. I also want to thank all of my friends who helped direct traffic, pass out gift bags, take pictures, and most importantly donate. Finally I want to thank the local police and fire departments for their participation. It was a fun afternoon for everyone involved.

Years ago I had a good friend who got involved in the financial planning business. In his previous life he was a Baptist preacher who I met during the days of building an Amway business. We became good friends and he played a huge part in helping me grow spiritually. After leaving the ministry and starting his financial planning business with John Hancock, he could see that it would be much more beneficial to own his own business rather than working for somebody else. He approached me about lending him $50,000 to start his business and set up an office. It felt great to give him the money to help him realize his dream.

I know the saying "never lend friends money" because a lot of times you don't get your money back and you lose a friend. In this case, I got my money back and helped a friend in need realize his dream. He built his business into a very large financial planning business managing over $100 million and had his own radio show and TV spot. Sadly, he passed away unexpectedly at fifty-six. I had no idea when I lent him the money the ramifications that would come from it. His wife was able to sell the business and never has to worry about money again. When she passes away, this money will be given to their children and create a legacy that could go on for generations. I never thought about what a huge impact it could have on so many people's lives. I was just trying to help out a friend.

On a lighter note, years ago I had a cousin who is a farmer who'd had a couple of tough years in the farming business. He is eight years older than me and we were the first generation off the farm. In the summers when we came back for family reunions, I would call him and we would do things city kids don't get to do like shoot guns, ride tractors, bale hay, and other fun farm things. Anyway, I knew he had a couple of tough years and he had two

young boys. I called him up and told him I had won a big football bet and made a couple thousand dollars (a story I made up). I told him I wanted him and his family to come to Myrtle Beach to visit me and I offered to pay for their airplane tickets. He reluctantly agreed as he is a proud person that wasn't looking for handouts. When they flew in, I rented a stretch limousine for the afternoon to pick them up and take them around Myrtle Beach. We had a blast! One thing led to another and we jumped in our conversion van to visit my parents in Orange Park, Florida. Well, when you're that close to Disney World, with a family with two small boys, you just have to go! We went for the day and had a great time. We worked our way back to Myrtle Beach, and they flew home a week later.

I had forgotten about this adventure when my cousin came to visit me in Myrtle Beach when he found out I had ALS. One morning while at the kitchen table, he came up to me with a piece of paper in his hand and handed it to me. There was a check made out to me for $1,500. He said he had a really good year in the farming business and he wanted to repay me for the trip to Disney World because at the time there was no way he could afford to take his kids on a trip like that. With tears in my eyes I told him I appreciated the gesture and that I would always keep the check but never cash it. To this day I have it tucked between my cell phone cover and the cell phone as a reminder of the great time we had together.

Another friend of mine who started his business right next door to my business when we were both in our twenties came to me a couple of years ago. He had taken some losses on some real estate deals he was involved with and didn't have money to pay his property taxes. We've been friends for over thirty years and it was very difficult for him to come and ask me for money. He said he would pay it back in just a few months. Those few months turned into many months. Then he paid me a little bit here and there when he could to pay down the debt. I told my wife that if I died before the debt was paid off, not to worry about it because over the years he had done so many things to help me out. It felt good not to worry about having to get paid back, but I will tell you he paid every dollar back and we're still great friends.

On another occasion I had a fellow realtor who had a friend with two girls who both had a rare form of cancer. It was their dream to spend a week in Myrtle Beach with their family. This particular realtor knew I owned two oceanfront condos (remember my bad investment?) and asked if there was anything I could do to help this family out. It felt so good to be able to let them stay in one of my condos for the whole week at no charge. Even though it was a bad investment, some good did come out of it. One of the girls has since passed away, but my fellow realtor told me they had the time of their lives and thanked me for helping make it possible. It feels good to help people less fortunate than yourself, maybe those you don't even know, and make their lives a little better. I was glad I was able to help out.

I have a younger brother and during the Internet boom I wanted to teach him the art of investing. Back in 2000, my parents gave each of us kids $5,000 for Christmas one year. I knew the $5,000 meant a lot more to him than it did to me at the time. I opened a brokerage account in both our names and put my $5,000 in the account that he was supposed to match by putting his $5,000 in too. Unfortunately, shortly after this the Internet bubble burst, and my $5,000 turned into $1,500. As you can imagine with him watching my investing prowess he was a

Craig with his sister and brothers

little reluctant to put his $5,000 to work. We both forgot about it for several years, but from time to time I would buy different stocks and over the years the account grew to a little over $20,000. I asked him when he was going to put his $5,000 in, and he said it's your money so do what you want with it. I took $10,000 out for my half and to recoup my original $5,000 and left the other $10,000 in the account. Since then, that $10,000 has grown to a little over $26,000. When I contracted ALS, I wasn't sure what to do with this account because technically it was my money, but the purpose of it was to help my younger brother and teach him about investing. I called him one day and told him that I didn't want this to be a burden on my wife when I passed away so we needed to do something with this money. Because I didn't really need it at the time, I felt very good about being able to assign the account to him and let him have it all. Hopefully he has learned how to make money grow in the stock market and will continue to keep his money invested to help him and his family one day.

There have been many smaller occasions that come to mind when it comes to giving. When my parents moved to Florida years ago, they moved into a mobile home park and I was able to buy them a golf cart to tool around in. When my wife's family members had some struggles it was a joy to be able to send them money for repairs of their properties or just to help them out.

Small gifts are wonderful, too. During a recent church service, the assistant pastor spoke about having a collection of Batman and Robin drinking glasses that were giveaways at McDon-

ald's back when he was a child. He was devastated when he
knocked the Robin glass off the table and it broke into pieces. As a
child he spoke about how he tried to glue the glass back together
with super glue and what a tragic event this had been in his life.
He brought the other three glasses to
the actual sermon that day. I don't
remember exactly what the sermon
was about but it broke my heart that
this was such a painful childhood
memory. When I got home that night,
I got on E-bay and found a set of four
Robin glasses and one Batman glass
for only about $35. I ordered them

and they came in the following week. I don't know who was more
excited, me for being able to repair his childhood memory or him
with the look on his face when I gave him the set of glasses. He
truly looked like a 35-year old kid on Christmas. Since then we
have become great friends. He has been over for numerous porch
visits and he even brought his wife along one time. We had a
blast. I didn't know Nathan very well before I gave him the Robin
glasses. The last time he came over we got into a bit of a deep dis-
cussion about whether or not his breaking that glass as a kid set
up a chain of events that led us to that porch visit thirty-two years
later. Who was the real benefactor in this one small act of kindness? I would say I benefitted way more.

Last Christmas I wanted to do something nice for my assistant. She's been there for me since before my diagnosis and right

through the writing of this book. I gave her a $5,000 Christmas bonus. I can't express what joy it gave me as her eyes filled with tears and she said, "I want to give you a great big hug." Unfortunately, because of Covid I was on the inside of the screen porch and she was on the outside.

So as you can see, whether it's helping a friend start a business, surprising somebody with a trip, or giving money away, the real secret of life is giving back and helping others. There is nothing that I have done in business that has given me greater joy than to be able to help others in need. One of my missions in writing this book is to carry on a legacy after I'm gone. From the proceeds of this book, 10% is going to be donated to the South Carolina ALS Association, and 10% is going to be donated to church and church-related activities. So I want to thank you for purchasing this book and knowing that part of the money is going to some very good causes.

Chapter 10: Look at How Lucky You Are

"This nation, under God, shall have a new birth of freedom; and that government of the people, by the people, for the people, shall not perish from the earth."
- Abraham Lincoln

"If ever a time should come, when vain and aspiring men shall possess the highest seats in Government, our country will stand in need of its experienced patriots to prevent its ruin."
- Samuel Adam

It absolutely disgusts me to the core when people say bad things about this country. It is by far the greatest country on the face of the planet and I'll prove it to you. People are risking their lives and their family's lives by the hundreds of thousands every month to just have a chance, not even a guarantee, to cross the border to become an American citizen. Think about that! We're not East Germany! We didn't build the wall on the southern border to keep people in!

By the way, here's a newsflash, we're not all equal! We aren't now, we weren't then, and we NEVER will be so quit your belly aching and get to work. I'll never have what Donald Trump has and my dad didn't leave me $50 million dollars when he died. Your job is to get off your ass and use whatever tools you have at whatever level you're at and make the world a better place for the next generation...THAT'S IT! If you hit it big, share it. Stop listening to people who tell you that you are owed something. You aren't owed anything. There are more opportunities now than in the history of the world.

I have a friend whose nephew just signed a five-year contract with the Los Angeles Clippers for $63 million dollars. That's over a million dollars a month or $250,000 a week and he doesn't even start. He averages about seven minutes a game and maybe five to seven points. In no other country in the world can you do that. You can live anywhere in this country you want including Hawaii, nobody will stop you.

I always find it funny when people move down to South Carolina from up North, which is about half my neighborhood. They always want to change things. Isn't it amazing that they are moving down to a state with beautiful weather, a conservative government, friendly people, and low taxes. Not to mention, the beautiful beaches, the lower cost of living, over one hundred golf courses in the area, and they want us to be more like them. I wonder how many neighborhoods up North are filled with people moving there from South Carolina.

I'm sorry, I got off on a bit of a tangent there. (I love ALL my Northern friends and you know who you are; just remember you moved here, we didn't move there.) Here's a hot tip: if you want to make somebody from South Carolina mad just say "that's not how we do it up north."

A friend of ours named Julie was my physical therapist. She called me one day after I had stopped therapy because of my condition and asked if I would do a Zoom call for her class so they could learn more about what a person goes through with ALS on a daily basis. I was more than happy to do it and my wife joined in. The class had prepared questions and I (being somewhat of a joker) ended up using the whole hour. A few days later, Julie brought me responses from her class on our back porch. I sat and read them and cried like a baby when I saw what an impact I had on their lives.

Julie said, "Craig and Katie chose to share their story of living and dying from ALS with those who may need it most. Nursing students from a nearby college probably received one of the best lessons in the humanity of medicine. However, they would also learn later the wisdom that is found from the one who is living while dying. I discovered this wisdom too as I read the second letter."

Here is the letter I wrote back to the class:

Think about how lucky you were to be born in America. America is the best country to be born. Two-hundred and forty-four years ago this country was founded upon a land that had nothing of what we see today. I'm sixty-two years old or roughly ¼ the age of this entire country. Think about that! During my lifetime we put a man on the moon, air travel is possible for the average person, we carry a super-computer on our hip and wear its counterpart as a watch. Some of the greatest achievements in history took place during my sixty-two years. People in this country have been able to create some of the greatest corporations in the world, like Boeing, Microsoft, Amazon, Apple, and Facebook! Imagine that!

People around the entire world fly OUR planes, use OUR software, buy OUR cell phones, and socialize on OUR Facebook! In your lifetime you will have self-driving cars and if you save, YOU will be able to travel to space as a private citizen. Heck, that will probably be in the next five years. Can you imagine what else you will witness during your lifetime?

Yes, we live in the best country in the whole world!

Don't feel sorry for me. I grew up in a great two-parent home with one sister and two brothers. My Dad was an engineer, so we moved...a lot. I lived in Ohio, Illinois, Michigan, Connecticut, Florida and even spent a couple of years in Venezuela, South America.

Somehow, I came to Myrtle Beach in 1982 and never left. I've been married to my wife, Katie, for 33 years this November. We have four great kids, all of whom graduated in the top eight or better in their class.

I've owned my own business most of my life. I've made and lost millions of dollars, I've owned fast cars and slow cars. I've met Mickey Mantle, Arnold Palmer, and even George Foreman. I've seen BB King, Diana Ross, and Taylor Swift in concert. I've flown on private jets and have ridden in limousines and even owned and flew my own airplane! I've been on cruises, more than I can count.

I've been to almost every state, even Hawaii. I've been to most of the Caribbean islands, and I've climbed the Great Wall of China.

PLEASE DON'T FEEL SORRY FOR ME!!!

I've had a great life! I'm just going to miss the fourth quarter!

What I found most interesting in reading your comments was how many of you made comments about how I helped put your life in perspective with comments 'life is short' and 'Craig inspired me to work even harder in life to reach my goals.' Others wrote, 'I won't take life for granted' or 'Life is precious, we should never waste it.' And also, 'It made me think there are no guarantees in life' and 'I need to appreciate it every day.' I was deeply moved by your comments.

But in reality, it is impossible to have a complete perspective until you look back. So, let me challenge you:

- Don't be average.
- Don't just get a job and do the same thing your entire life. Remember, you live in the greatest country in the world and you can do and be anything you want to be.
- Don't settle.
- Dream BIG!
- Make a bucket list and start working on it...TODAY!
- Go hot air ballooning, snow skiing in Vail, see the Grand Canyon, look over the edge of the Hoover dam, party in Vegas once...or twice, scuba dive with the great white sharks of Australia, or jump out of a plane...with a parachute!

- You can do ANYTHING you want to do, and you only have to imagine it.

Finally, you may not think about this much, but we all have the same EXIT strategy. No one gets out alive and none of us will truly know when. Even with ALS, I don't know for sure and neither did my doctors, if they did you would be reading a dead man's writing now.

A friend lent me a book called *Proof of Heaven* written by Eben Alexander. I suggest you all read it. I imagine everyone dying begins to wonder about what is next and wouldn't we all like a little proof. I challenge you to start seeking truth and not proof. When you seek truth and ask for faith, then that will provide the proof that you need. More importantly, by starting now it will change your entire life.

For myself, I looked at my children as babies and marveled at the miracle of creation. From my back porch I now watch the big black starry sky and wonder what's out there and how big is our universe? I realize with full confidence that there is something way, way BIGGER than us that created us, and I am thankful for our Creator's imagination.

So, in your life, take the time to look at the stars, think about the incredible human body, get right with God and realize all of us are here for a very short time...it's what's next is where it REALLY GETS GOOD!

Thanks again for all your heartfelt comments. See...I told you this damn disease will show you the great side of humanity.

You've proved it to me again with all your comments. Look me up in the next life or come for a Porch Visit anytime.

Craig

Chapter 11: Get Your Life Right with God...or Else!

"Faith gives you an inner strength and a sense of balance and perspective in life"
- Gregory Peck

I am going to give you the order of importance on how you should prioritize what's really important in your life. But I'm going to do it in reverse order starting with the least important.

#4. Your job: It has always amazed how so many people go to a job they don't like in this great country. C'mon people, why in this world would you do something to make a living that you dread doing? Find something that you enjoy doing and go after that. A job is a means to an end. It should allow you to keep a roof over your head and food in your belly while using what you have learned in this book to save and invest until you make enough money to pursue your passion in life. Don't let a job trap you in a rut you can never escape from.

I lost focus in my life too often and spent too much time on my career and ignoring my family and spiritual life. I got out of balance. Ask yourself a few questions and reflect on if your answers are positive. The hourglass of life isn't slowing down.

- Do I enjoy what I'm doing?
- Is this job going to get me where I need to be to reach my goal?
- Can I move up at my own pace?
- Is the compensation enough for my responsibilities?

If the answer isn't yes then don't quit your job but start looking for something that will meet your criteria.

#3. **Your country:** I already told you about what a great country this is in previous chapters. I know I'm going to sound like an old man here but somehow this country has jumped off its rails. When I grew up, great inventions were celebrated and the men and women behind these ideas were heroes. From Henry Ford and the automobile to the Wright brothers and the airplane to Amelia Earhart flying across the ocean to Neil Armstrong who risked his life to be the first man on the moon. The country celebrated the risk these people took by throwing ticker tape parades to celebrate them as they dared to do what no one had done before.

What happened? How come we're not giving ticker tape parades to Jeff Bezos or Elon Musk or Bill Gates? Why aren't we putting these people on a pedestal and cheering them on? Isn't your life better with Amazon? Doesn't your computer work better with software? Self driving cars are just around the corner. No pun intended.

Only in America. Somewhere along the way rather than celebrating these people who literally changed the world and how we live, we started to hear that it's not fair that they have so much and so many people have so little.

Wealthy people are being vilified, success is a bad thing. You hear "no one should have more than a billion dollars," or "it's not fair that so few have so much while others have so little."

Wrong...if you don't like people being successful then cancel your Amazon account, throw your laptop and iPhone off a bridge, and ride a horse home for Thanksgiving. No one is holding a gun to your head and making you buy these goods and services. I can tell you that these people can figure out how to allocate the money so much better than the government. You know how I know? If they make the wrong decision they go out of business, so they are really careful about where every penny goes.

Our national debt is approaching 30 trillion dollars. That is how you don't manage money properly. One day that amount is going to be so large that we won't be able to make the minimum payment. It will cause a lot of pain. Giving someone something for nothing doesn't do anything to help a personal self image. In fact I believe it hurts your self image. Remember how good you felt the first time you rode a bike or got your learners permit to drive a car or the day you made your solo flight on your way to getting your pilot's license? You felt like you were king of the world. You could do anything.

Never ever vote for someone who wants to take from the rich to give to the poor because politicians feel they know more than an achiever. It never works. Let them create a business and create jobs and create wealth for their employees and make the world a better place to live in. Then I'll be impressed. Without a country we have nothing.

#2. **Family:** I was lucky enough to be brought up in a loving and supportive family. Family is the ultimate fallback position for many people. Friends can come and go, but family is always there from the beginning.

Growing up all over the world it was always a great thrill every year to come back to Ohio for the Dierksheide family reunion to meet and see the generations of aunts, uncles, grandparents, cousins, and sometimes even extended family from Germany would show up. I always thought of Ohio as my home even though I actually only lived there for the first few years of my life.

I have such great memories of going to Bowling Green for the National Tractor Pull. Or the county fair to watch the greased pig contest where young kids would chase greased pigs in a pen and try to catch them for prizes. Or the cow pie contest where the local

high school football field was sectioned off into one hundred
equal squares and you could bet on as many squares as you like,
then a well fed cow is turned loose to graze until he poops and if
you're lucky enough to have picked that square...you win! Great
memories.

I remember talking about where I wanted to be buried with
my cousin and he was flabbergasted when I said, "right here in
Ohio." He said, "but you didn't even grow up here." Family.

#1. God: THE most important of the four by far. It has always
amazed me how people have so much faith that they will jump in
a car and drive cross country, or have the faith to get on an airplane and fly across the ocean to Hawaii without even knowing
who is flying the plane, or stand on the top of a mountain on a
pair of skis and have the faith that they're going to make it to the
bottom without breaking every bone in their body. Forget about
those people who parachute, hang glide, bungee jump, or rock
climb.

How can people have so much faith when they do all those
crazy things and yet when they look at the miracle of birth or the
vastness of the universe, they don't have faith in God? I just don't
understand it! When I go to the doctor's office and look at the
posters on the wall of the human body it never ceases to amaze
me all the different parts from the skeletal system, the muscles,
the blood, and the heart that keeps the blood flowing, awake or
asleep. And what about the inner ear and how it allows you to

stand upright. Not to mention the brain and the memory and sub-conscious mind.

All from a single cell...say what?

The evidence of intelligent design is amazing and all around us! Scientist Stephen Meyer, PhD once said the more we learn about DNA, the more it speaks to the fact that there must be an intelligent creator. He stated, "whenever you find a sequential arrangement that's complex and corresponds to an independent pattern or function requirement, the kind of information is always the product of intelligence...the presence of this type of information in DNA also implies an intelligent source." (Meyer is quoted in Lee Strobel, *The Case for the Creator*, Zondervan, 2006/2014, page 294).

I remember when we had our twins after four years of infertility. I would hold them in my arms for hours and wonder how the eyebrows knew how to grow only above the eyes, or how and why the two lines under your nose knew to form there? Why is your whole head not covered with hair? And the holes! How does your nose know to connect to your lungs, how do your ears know to connect to your brain so you can hear and how does your mouth connect with your throat and intestines all in one long tube with openings on both ends? These are the questions that have kept people awestruck for centuries. Even the author of Psalm 139 expresses this same kind of wonder when he says, "For You formed my inmost being; You knit me together in my mother's womb. I praise you because I am fearfully and wonderfully made."

When I sit in my backyard and gaze out into eternity wondering what's out there, where does it end?

As I sit here typing on my phone with the side of my thumb as my muscles deteriorate, I am kind of watching the process in reverse. I tell people who ask that ALS is like dying in slow motion...fast! Every day I can't do what I did the day before. It's getting harder to talk, I choke a lot, my fingers are curling, I must be lifted to be put in bed or go to the bathroom. It's a horrible way to die. There is a great example about this in the story of the sisters Mary and Martha and their encounter with Jesus from Luke 10:38-42 which says,

As Jesus and his disciples were on their way, he came to a village where a woman named Martha opened her home to him. She had a sister called Mary, who sat at the Lord's feet listening to what he said. But Martha was distracted by all the preparations that had to be made. She came to him and asked, "Lord, don't you care that my sister has left me to do the work by myself? Tell her to help me!"

"Martha, Martha," the Lord answered, "you are worried and upset about many things, but few things are needed – or indeed only one. Mary has chosen what is better, and it will not be taken away from her."

In this story, Martha is so busy making preparations that she misses the incredible opportunity in front of her…the chance to spend time with Jesus. It is so easy to be busy and to equate busyness with importance, but sometimes busyness keeps us from seeing the incredible things right in front of us and knocks our priorities out of whack. That's why I think it's so important to step back and look at our priorities.

On the bright side, I used to go one hundred miles an hour seven days a week until this disease slowed me down. Probably like most of you are doing now! I would never wish this disease on anyone…unless…that's what it takes for YOU to slow down enough to develop a personal relationship with Jesus.

John 3:16 For God so loved the world that he gave his one and only Son, that whoever believes in him shall not perish but have eternal life. [17] For God did not send his Son into the world to condemn the world, but to save the world through him. [18] Whoever believes in him is not condemned.

Editor's Note: Craig Dale Dierksheide passed away Friday, March 4, 2022, after a valiant three and a half year battle with ALS (Lou Gehrig's Disease) at the age of 63. He worked so hard on this book and had just finished his final round of editing prior to publication. Craig was an amazing son, brother, husband, dad, uncle, father-in-law, friend, and now author.

At least 10% of the proceeds from this book will be donated to:
The ALS Association South Carolina Chapter
130 Gardeners Circle
PMB 622
Johns Island, SC 29455.
803-851-3233
or visit: www.scalsa.org

Made in United States
Orlando, FL
09 April 2022

16670308R00078